You Can't
God Can

You Can't
God Can

Making a Difference in Your World

Mike Lee

Alive Book Publishing

You Can't God Can
Making a Difference in Your World
Copyright © 2018 by Mike Lee

Additional copies may be ordered from the publisher for educational,
business, promotional or premium use.
For information, contact ALIVE Book Publishing at:
alivebookpublishing.com, or call (925) 837-7303.

Book Design by Alex Johnson
Quotes from the Bible are from the New International Version (NIV).

ISBN 13
978-1-63132-050-7

ISBN 10
1-63132-050-5

Library of Congress Control Number: 2018939999

Library of Congress Cataloging-in-Publication Data
is available upon request.

First Edition

Published in the United States of America by ALIVE Book Publishing
and ALIVE Publishing Group, imprints of Advanced Publishing LLC
3200 A Danville Blvd., Suite 204, Alamo, California 94507
alivebookpublishing.com

PRINTED IN THE UNITED STATES OF AMERICA

10 9 8 7 6 5 4 3 2 1

Dedication

There's an old saying, "Behind every successful pastor is a wife that is as shocked as he is." There's no way there would be Hope Community Church without the support of my wife, Laura. Even when I didn't have confidence in myself, she had confidence in me and the vision that God called us to. Laura not only supported me but built one of the best Family Ministries in the United States.

I also want to thank my sons, Aaron and Adam, for all their support through the years. It's tough to grow up at church! Today they both work on staff and bring joy to my life.

Table of Contents

Foreword

By the grace of God, this past year the Triangle (Raleigh-Durham) was home to five of *Outreach Magazine's* "Fastest Growing Churches in America." But of the five on that list, Pastor Mike Lee was here long before the rest of us, building a movement devoted to bringing people who are far from God to an encounter with the life-changing message of Jesus Christ. God used Pastor Mike as the gospel pioneer in this area, his forerunner to till up the soil, sow gospel seed far and wide, birth kingdom vision, and create a thirst for genuine encounters with God in one of the fastest growing areas of America.

Pastor Mike's messages, like this book, are filled with wisdom, gritty authenticity, humor, earthy practicality, and genuine gospel power. The most frequent word I hear when people tell me about their experience at Hope Community Church is "life-change." They say this, more often than not, with tears in their eyes, as they talk about how God used Mike's messages to interrupt their lives and introduce them to God. I can't think of any way I'd rather be described.

I have personally benefited in numerous ways—both direct and indirect—from Pastor Mike's ministry. The church he's led now for more than two decades helped foster a gospel hunger that has permeated the Triangle. He has promoted a spirit of unity and gospel cooperation among like-minded pastors. Most of the Triangle pastors I know I have met at an event hosted by Hope Community.

On a personal level, Mike has always opened up his life to

me, sharing his wisdom, experiences, and even Hope's resources with us. And he has demonstrated that rare quality of caring more about the kingdom than his particular church. I have had the privilege of serving in his shadow, reaping the benefits of his labor.

As you'll see in this book, one thing moves Mike's heart more than any other—seeing people transformed by the grace of God. Jesus said, "There will be more rejoicing in heaven over one sinner who repents than over ninety-nine righteous persons who do not need to repent" (Luke 15:7 NIV). That's an amazing statement, and one every Christian leader should wrestle with. Of all the things to get excited about in the body of Christ, and of all the things to focus our attention on, one above them all brings joy to God's heart—seeing lost people come home. Pastor Mike has made a lifetime of seeing this happen. In these pages, you get to learn from a master fisherman sharing his secrets with you.

The stories contained in this book will not only instruct you; they will inspire you to see things like this happen through your life, too. I've heard it said that some books take a year to write, while others take a lifetime. This book is one of the latter. In this book you'll see how God used an ordinary man to accomplish extraordinary things in the lives of very unlikely people—and how he wants to do the same in you. Buckle your seatbelt. I assure you that you won't be the same after reading it.

Pastor Mike is not that much older than me. But I do consider him a mentor, example, and friend, a leader of extraordinary gifting and wisdom—to whom I, along with thousands of other believers in the Triangle and around the world, owe a great debt of gratitude. You'll feel the same when you finish this book.

—J.D. Greear, Ph.D.
Pastor, Summit Church
North Carolina

Introduction

You've Got the Wrong Guy!

Years ago, I was sitting in a meeting at the Leadership Network in Dallas, Texas, with nine other pastors, all of whom I consider to be very successful. As I looked around the room, I wasn't sure why I had been invited. To be perfectly honest, I've never felt comfortable around pastors, especially successful ones. For me, being in the same meeting with these guys was like putting whipped cream on an onion. In my mind, I seemed out of place; I didn't fit. They were brilliant, cutting-edge leaders, conference speakers, and published authors. They had huge congregations. And they had hair!

It didn't help my insecurities when the guest facilitator made his opening statement, "Every successful pastor has two things in common: a strong calling to the ministry and a strong mentor."

I sat there thinking, "Great! I'm already 0 for 2, and we just started." But it was just another reminder that Laura and I are probably the most unlikely couple in the world to be used by God to accomplish what He has accomplished through Hope Community Church.

My education is sketchy at best. I don't get very excited about speaking at places other than Hope. Until now, I'd never written a book, never felt "called" to ministry, and no one had ever mentored me. Heck, I grew up thinking that I never wanted to be in ministry. In fact, the one thing I was sure of when I sat in church as a child was that being a pastor had to be the worst job in the world. While everyone else was enjoying the weekend at the beach or the mountains or the lake, a pastor had to be at church

. . . every Sunday! That did not fit with my plan for my life.

My dream was to be a football coach. *My* plan was to start wherever I could get a break, then work my way up through the ranks until I was coaching on Sunday afternoons! It was the only career I could imagine would top being at the beach or the mountains or the lake or any other place on a Sunday. However, it says in Proverbs 16:9: "In their hearts humans plan their course, but the Lord establishes their steps."

After college, on schedule to fulfill my plan for my life, I was able to land a job as a teacher and coach. I was on my way. But toward the end of the school year, a small church that we were attending in Southern California asked me to leave teaching and become their Youth Minister. Laura and I had been working with the students as volunteers and we really enjoyed being a part of what God was doing in their lives, so I thought, "How bad can it be? I'd have to teach Sunday School for an hour each week, but then I'd get to spend the rest of my time at the beach playing volleyball and roasting hot dogs!" Plus, if I didn't like it, I could always return to teaching and coaching. After all, I wasn't "called" to ministry. I accepted the position.

After a few months in my new role, our Senior Pastor was forced to step down because of health issues. The Elder Board invited me to my first elder meeting and asked me if I would be willing to also take on the role of Interim Teaching Pastor until they found a new Senior Pastor for the church. From my perspective, it didn't seem like that big of a deal. Teaching was teaching. I had filled in on a couple of Sundays when the pastor had been away and no one had thrown anything at me. I took it as a good sign. Add to that the fact that I was young and stupid. I accepted the challenge. I can still remember what it was like to finish teaching Sunday School and then make the quick transition to the adults.

Over the next few months, the church saw some significant growth and people seemed to be happy. I was invited to my second elder meeting. I assumed that it was to inform me that they had found a new senior pastor for the church. Instead, they asked me if I would consider taking the position permanently. My emotions were all over the place. It looked like becoming a pastor was about to become a reality. I was willing to consider the offer only because the half-dozen men that made up the Elder Team were six of the godliest and most mature Christian men I've ever known to this day. Plus, if I didn't like it I could always go back to teaching and coaching. Remember, I was never "called" to ministry.

Laura and I prayed about it for a few days, and I accepted the job as Senior Pastor for the church. I was only 24 and Laura was 21. I immediately enrolled in seminary and took some classes; at the same time, I tried to figure out what I was supposed to be doing as a Senior Pastor. I've now been in this role for over thirty-six years, yet I'm still not sure that I've ever been "called" to ministry, I've still never had a mentor, and I still don't know what I'm doing. God, indeed, has a sense of humor!

Laura's resume isn't very impressive either. She dropped out of college to marry me when I was 22 and she was 19. She had our first son at the mature age of 21 and our second son when she was barely 24. She taught music in Christian schools for nine years without a degree. After moving from California to Cary, North Carolina to start Hope Community Church, she transitioned to corporate work to help support the family. God rewarded her immensely which allowed me to work part-time construction while trying to start the church on the side. That was 1994.

We started Hope with five families on Easter Sunday that same year, and twenty-four years later, we have over 18,000 people that consider one of our campuses their church home. By the world's criteria, Laura and I are the most unlikely candidates for our job (again, like whipped cream on an onion). The fact that God chose us makes no sense whatsoever from a human perspective. But that's what this book is about. It's the story of what God has taught us over the years about how God can use us. What we've learned may surprise you; it will definitely encourage you.

My motivation for writing is simple: It's to encourage those who are followers of Jesus to start thinking a little bigger and ask the question, "God, what could you do through me if I could get my priorities and values lined up with your priorities and values?"

Some are already on that journey; some are already in the process of being utilized by God in incredible ways. Others have never thought of themselves as those who could make a significant impact in God's Kingdom. My message is simple: "If God could use us, why not you?"

I hope you will let God work in your heart and mind while reading this book. I pray that God will reveal to you the ways that you can make an impact in this world and in the lives of the people that God has placed around you. By the end of our time together, I hope you will "take the hill" with us as we turn the world, not upside down, but right side up with the Gospel of Jesus Christ.

Chapter 1
Not Me!

I pastor a big church. And just like any big church, we have thousands of people who've never considered the possibility that God can use them in significant and purposeful ways. My guess is that the average person who attends Hope represents the average church attendee in most of the average churches around the world.

We all have our reasons why we think our potential in God's Kingdom is limited. Maybe we're from a dysfunctional background and our family life was a disaster, so we naturally assume that God could never use us to make a difference in someone else's life or in His Kingdom.

Maybe we've been involved in some spectacular sinning. Our mission statement at Hope is to "Love people where they are and encourage them to grow in their relationship with Jesus Christ." It's a mission statement that I'm especially proud of because as a church of "messed-up" people, we do a pretty good job of living our mission. Over the years, God has put us to the test by bringing some individuals to our church that could, even by our standards, be considered "All-Pro" sinners. Maybe you believe you fall into that category.

Maybe you've just begun a relationship with God and you're taking baby steps in your spiritual journey — and "three steps forward and two steps back" describes your Christian walk. Or maybe you're still stepping out of one mess only to step right into another. We've all been there. At such a beginning stage of your spiritual journey, you can't even imagine how God could possibly use you. As a novice; there's so much to learn. In fact, you may have recently found the maps in the back of the Bible and secretly hope that I'll reference the "Book of Maps" because it's the one book you can locate.

Maybe you're at the other end of the spectrum—been around church for years. That's my story. I can't remember a time when I wasn't in church. I'm pretty sure that I was born in the choir loft. My church week consisted of Sunday School, Sunday morning service, Sunday afternoon choir practice, Sunday night service, Sunday night youth service after the Sunday night service, Wednesday night prayer meeting, and Thursday night visitation and soul-winning. On top of that, I was a bus captain! Those of you who lived through the Jack Hyles and Jerry Falwell era know what I'm talking about. The rest of you should pause and offer up a little prayer of thanksgiving to God that you were spared. But, again, maybe your story sounds like mine: You attended AWANA; you can name all the books of the Bible in perfect order; you've memorized a thousand Bible verses, all from the *KJV*; you've taken every class your church has to offer; you know your spiritual gifts, you've taken Strength-Finder (by the way, I have the gift of WOO—Winning Others Over—that will come into play later); you've memorized the "Romans Road" and are always prepared to share the hope that's in you; and you're a certified Stephen's minister. No matter which topic your pastor addresses, it's never deep enough for you— because you even know what really happened to the lost tribes of Israel. You've pretty much spent your life becoming a professional Christian. Yet as you look back over your journey, you find yourself wondering, "I have a lot of knowledge, but have I ever made a difference for God and His Kingdom?"

Or maybe you find yourself in a season of life where your total focus is on you, your education, your family, and your career. In other words, it's all about you. And for that reason, you haven't taken the time to explore the possibility of what God could do *through* you.

Regardless of where you are on your spiritual journey, have you ever slowed down long enough to ask, "God, what could you possibly use me to accomplish and how can I make an impact in someone's life?"

The reason those questions are so important is that there is no greater joy in life than realizing that God has used you to impact His Kingdom by changing another's spiritual destiny. Nothing else comes close.

Think about it, every incredible experience eventually loses its sizzle and becomes a memory. For example, I've had a great life and had a lot of wonderful experiences. I've had the pleasure of traveling to London, Paris, Rome, and Prague. I've fished for salmon in Alaska and for muskies on the French River in Canada. I had the opportunity to speak at a conference on Margarita Island off the coast of Venezuela (be honest, the name alone makes you want to visit there). I've partied with the pygmies in the Central African Republic rainforest. I've had the privilege of dedicating a worship center in Northern Uganda that our church built for an orphan village. In fact, as I'm writing this chapter, Laura and I are on a plane heading to Hawaii for my summer study break. My point is, I've had the opportunity to travel to some incredible places and meet some incredible people. Still, it pales when compared to the opportunity to be God's servant.

Even fancy cars cannot compete with serving God. For example, when I was a twelve-year-old, dirt-poor kid growing up in Durham, North Carolina, I saw my first Corvette and thought, "One day, I'm going to own one of those." But years later, when I finally got to the place in life where I could actually afford a Corvette, I learned an important lesson: By the time I could afford a Corvette, I was too old to get in and out of it! Plus, most church congregations aren't overly excited about their pastor looking like the neighborhood drug dealer as he drives around the community in his flashy muscle car. And so, I decided to do what any respectable minister would do. Instead of getting a Corvette, I decided to get a Harley.

After I took care of all of the preliminary issues like getting tattoos and going through the safety classes, I walked into Laura's office and boldly proclaimed that I was getting a Harley Davidson motorcycle. But, there was one thing I hadn't planned on. I hadn't planned on Laura boldly proclaiming in return, "Motorcycles are too dangerous. With my luck, you'll get into an accident and instead of it killing you, I'll be stuck taking care of you for the rest of your life. There's no way that's ever going to happen!" (As you'll learn in this book, Laura is a very pragmatic person.)

Well, I wasn't ready to give up my motorcycle dream so easily. In fact, I thought, "No problem. I have the gift of WOO (I told you it would come into play). I'll wear her down, and I'll win her over." I began to talk about motorcycles incessantly. I never went more than an hour without bringing up the topic. I pointed out every motorcycle I saw going down the road. I described in great detail the motorcycle I was going to buy. I would take Laura to showrooms so she could see the beautiful chrome and hear the loud pipes. I would try on leather chaps so she could see how sexy I looked in them. I was 100% confident that my incredible charm would change her mind, until she snapped.

"You will never, never, ever, ever, over my dead body, get a motorcycle!" she said in a tone totally unacceptable for someone who is in the esteemed role of a pastor's wife.

And then she paused and said out of frustration, "You've always wanted a Corvette. Why don't you get a Corvette?"

Well, hello! I'm all about mutual submission when it comes to marriage, especially when it benefits me. And if Laura insists I get a Corvette, then I must submit! So, I went right out and purchased my first Corvette. It was old—the seats were ripped, the glass top had a crack in it, and when I turned the headlights on, more often than not, only one of the lights would pop up; in fact, I nicknamed the car "Mr. Winky." But even with all of its imperfections, I absolutely loved my Corvette. I would crawl into the driver's seat, turn the key, the engine would come to life, and the exhaust would rumble. Exhilarating! But do you know what? Over time, it got less and less exhilarating, and it lost its sizzle and eventually, I got rid of it.

Let me give another example. Have you ever moved into what you considered to be your dream home? Remember counting down the days until it was ready for you to occupy? Laura and I went on this adventure. The day we moved in, we made everyone take their shoes off at the front door and no one was allowed to take food outside of the kitchen area; we didn't want any spills. It was our goal to keep the house pristine and perfect.

However, that year there was a problem: It was our turn to host Laura's side of the family for Thanksgiving. And when Laura's family is together, chaos ensues—a small world war. It's noisy, things get broken, food ends up in places that it should never be. To avoid the trauma, I suggested that we tell everyone we were going away for Thanksgiving and then hide in a room with the lights out, but Laura vetoed my idea, and I had to accept the reality that there was nothing I could do about it.

Thanksgiving Day finally arrived and everyone showed up. The noise quickly grew to a roar. There was food, laughter, football—it was another awesome holiday with family. Eventually, everyone drifted away until Laura and I were left alone in our dream house with only a few casualties and minimal damage.

I'm not sure when it happened, but at some point, between Thanksgiving and Christmas, our house quit being a dream, and it became a home. Nobody takes off their shoes and leaves them by the door when they visit. Nobody stays in the kitchen when they eat. When family comes over, I say, "The more, the merrier." It's just another house. And that's the way it is with things of this world—the sizzle wears off.

People are different from things. When I think back over my life and the people that God has used me to impact in a spiritual way, I cannot talk about them without getting emotional. I feel how the Apostle Paul must have felt about Timothy.

I'll never forget when I first met Pat. He was in a hospital after a crack cocaine overdose. His wife contacted me through a friend who attended our church. She asked if I would visit him, and I did. While kneeling alongside Pat on the cold, hard hospital floor, Pat invited Jesus into his life to be his Savior.

The problem was that he was still a crack addict, and as a result, I ended up spending a lot of time with Pat. While I was starting a church, I needed to make a living, so for a period of time, I helped Pat in his concrete business. It worked out well for me to be close to him and hold him accountable. There were a couple of times when Pat's drug dealer called me and I had to go by the ATM and withdraw enough cash to pay off the debt he had run up and get him out of the crack house.

It's now been over fifteen years since the night that I prayed with Pat on that hospital floor. Thanks to God's grace and power, he's been clean and sober for years, yet I still get chills every time I see him. The reason? Because when God uses you to impact someone's life in a way that alters their eternal destiny, you never forget it. When God uses you to impact someone's life to break the chains that shackled that person and they can now move forward in their new journey with Christ, it leaves an impression that cannot be compared to anything else. The excitement, the joy of those experiences never, ever goes away.

Some of you are thinking, "That's what I want to experience; that's how I want to live my life!" But it seems that when we begin to think that way, it's only a matter of time before Satan, the great accuser, shows up in our lives and reminds us of all the reasons why that life will never become a reality. Well, I want to prove Satan wrong! I want you to experience that joy, and I want you to experience it often. And so, as we go on this journey together, I pray that you will grasp what God can do through you if you will allow him.

I know what some of you are thinking, "That sounds good. Sign me up . . . I'm all in . . . let's do it! Not only is the flesh willing, the spirit is strong!" Then you recall your past, all of your failures and baggage, your screw-ups and mistakes. You look at others at church or in your small group and from your perspective, everybody else looks like they have it together. Everybody has it all...except you. And your very next thought is, "Yeah, maybe God can use them in a significant way to impact His Kingdom, but I don't think that's ever going to be a reality in my life." I get that; I'm human, too. In fact, your pastor may not tell you this, so I will. Pastors are no different than you. We have a past. We've failed. We have baggage. We still screw-up. Often our faith is weak and we struggle with doubts about God's ability to use us, too.

The reason we all think this way is because of the natural tendency to evaluate our potential by the world's criteria. However, what we discover in the Bible is that the things that make a person useful in God's Kingdom are completely different from the things that make a person useful on planet Earth. We find that what success looks like from God's perspective is totally different than what success looks like from the world's perspective.

You can see an example of this in one of my favorite stories from the Bible. If you're familiar with the Old Testament, you know that when God established the Nation of Israel, He decided not to give Israel a human king. Instead, God would be their king. In other words, it was a theocracy, not a monarchy. By the way, that's not a bad plan. I mean, don't you think our nation would be better off if God was our King?

Anyway, even though God himself was the King of Israel, the people of Israel wanted to be like all the other nations. They wanted a king they could actually see and touch. They wanted him to have a throne, wear a robe, wear a crown. I'm sure they got tired of explaining to surrounding nations, "We have a king; you just can't see him."

But God speaks to His prophet, Samuel, and tells him, "Now listen to them; but warn them solemnly and let them know what the king who will reign over them will claim as his rights" (1 Samuel 8:9).

And so, in the next several verses Samuel tells the people what God said.

> "This is what the king who will reign over you will claim as his rights: He will take your sons and make them serve with his chariots and horses, and they will run in front of his chariots. Some he will assign to be commanders of thousands and commanders of fifties, and others to plow his ground and reap his harvest, and still others to make weapons of war and equipment for his chariots. He will take your daughters to be perfumers and cooks and bakers. He will take the best of your fields and vineyards and olive groves and give them to his attendants. He will take a tenth of your grain and of your vintage and give it to his officials and attendants. Your male and female servants and the best of your cattle and donkeys he will take for his own use. He will take a tenth of your flocks, and you yourselves will become his slaves. When that day comes, you will cry out for relief from the king you have chosen, but the Lord will not answer you in that day." (1 Samuel 8:11-18)

But even with Samuel's warning:

> "...the people refused to listen to Samuel. "No!" they said. "We want a king over us. Then we will be like all the other nations, with a king to lead us and to go out before us and fight our battles." When Samuel heard all that the

people said, he repeated it before the Lord. The Lord answered, 'Listen to them and give them a king.'" (1 Samuel 8:19-22)

So, the people of Israel began their search for a king, and they chose a man who was very impressive: Saul. If you want to go by externals, Saul was the guy, the obvious choice. According to 1 Samuel 9:2, he was tall, handsome, and probably dark. He appeared to have it together. My guess is that Saul was the kind of guy you would pick to marry your daughter if you are basing it on the things of this world.

Since he had all the markings of greatness, Saul was elected to be the first king of Israel. But by the time you get to 1 Samuel 16, God has absolutely had it with Saul, and it was because Saul made the classic leadership mistake. He thought that God had chosen him to be king because he looked like a king. He thought that God had chosen him to be the king because of his impressive pedigree. He thought that God had chosen him to be king because he had such incredible leadership skills, talents, and abilities. So naturally, when he became king, he relied on those things—looks, pedigree, leadership skills, talent, and ability—to get things done. And because he relied on his strengths instead of relying on God, he failed. Consequently, God decided that it was time for a new king in Israel and told Samuel to go down to the city of Bethlehem to the house of a man named Jesse.

When Samuel and his posse arrived, Samuel saw Eliab, Jesse's oldest son, and thought, "Surely the Lord's anointed stands here before the Lord." He thought, "He's tall, dark and handsome. He even looks like a king. This has got to be the guy." In other words, Samuel was getting ready to make the same mistake the Nation of Israel made when they chose Saul to be king. He was basing the choice on the things that impress us.

But God says to Samuel, "Do not consider his appearance or his height, for I have rejected him. The Lord does not look at the things people look at. People look at the outward appearance, but the Lord looks at the heart" (1 Samuel 16:7). In other words, the things that impress God are different than the things that impress us.

We have a really cool couple at Hope: Matt and Shannon. They're the kind of couple that, like Saul, really stand out in a crowd. They're both tall. They're both young. They're both attractive. They're both in incredible physical shape. In other words, they're both everything I'm not.

One weekend before a service, I was hanging out in the atrium when I spotted them. I walked over, struck up a conversation, and discovered why they stuck out so much: They were both models! Matt had been one of the lead male models for Abercrombie and Fitch and Shannon had starred in the first season of America's Next Top Model, which led to a modeling career. I told them that I would love to hear their story. That evening, Shannon sent me an email which illustrated the kind of person for whom God is looking. Shannon wrote:

> *Ever since I was a little girl I had always dreamed of becoming a supermodel. The Lord totally blew my mind when He brought this desire to life. My passion for modeling was intense, but my love for my Lord and Savior Jesus Christ consumed me like a raging fire. I had settled in my heart when I was a young girl that I would obey, follow, and serve Him at ALL costs. I had 'non-negotiables' in modeling. Things I would not do, no matter how much money or fame I would get from doing them. One of the things I decided was that I would save myself for marriage and my husband. The Lord tested me several times to see if my desire to please Him was greater than my desire to please the world. The Lord brought me face-to-face with lots of money, fame, notoriety, status, but by His amazing grace I did not cave. I knew those things wouldn't satisfy the deep longing in my soul that was made for Him. I knew that He had opened the door in the first*

place, so I needed to remain faithful to Him. It wasn't always easy, but it was worth it. There is nothing worth selling your soul for.

I trusted God with my life. I knew He was real. I knew His power. I knew He could do more than I could ever imagine, if I would trust Him. It wasn't easy trusting Him to bring my husband into my life because it seemed like He was taking forever! I chatted with God a few times about how long He seemed to be taking. I imagined Him smiling back while saying, 'If you saw what I had in store, you would see it will be worth the wait.' Little did I know the Lord would be sending me a man who also modeled and had the biggest campaign to date for Abercrombie and Fitch. He was featured in all kinds of magazines and had worked on shoots with supermodels including Adriana Lima and Elle McPherson. But do you know what stands out about him more than all that: It's his character; it's his humble heart; it's his desire to please Jesus. My focus on his looks faded and his heart captivated me to the core. He gave up thousands of dollars because his desire to please the Lord was greater. And if I wasn't blown away already by the Lord, I was about to be. Come to find out, Matthew had saved himself for marriage too! Here you have a male model that has girls just throwing themselves at him all the time, but he is choosing to wait. I could never put into words how much that meant to me. All of those prayers, lonely nights, agonizing days, were swallowed up with joy. We were able to give each other something on our wedding night that we chose to give no one else. I had always imagined that the Lord wrapped me like a beautiful package. Where the bow was perfectly placed, it hadn't been tossed around, and the edges not torn. I wanted to be that perfect package for my spouse.

The Lord had His watchful eye on us both. He had His guiding hand on our lives. Not because we are something 'special,' but because we CHOSE to keep Him first no matter what the cost. Serving the Lord will always cost you something, but it is always worth it.

I love that story, but it's more than a great story. It's a re-minder that the things that impress God are different from the things that impress mankind. It's a reminder that God looks into the heart and at the character of two young people who decide to put principle above money and worldly success. Why is that so important? Because what often causes us to question whether or not God can use us is that we tend to evaluate ourselves by a standard that God never established. God has a totally different standard. In other words, if you're thinking that you are going to do great things for God because you have the talent, the re-sume, the degree, the pedigree, and the looks, you're wrong. On the other hand, you may be thinking, "I don't have many gifts or talents. I can't sing or teach. I don't have a degree. I'm not all that impressive physically. I have a dysfunctional family background. There's no way that God could ever use me to do great things." But God has an entirely different criterion. Remember, the Lord does not look at the things that people look at.

Let's pick up the story in 1 Samuel 16.

"Then Jesse called Abinadab and had him pass in front of Samuel. But Samuel said, 'The Lord has not chosen this one either.' Jesse then had Shammah pass by, but Samuel said, 'Nor has the Lord chosen this one.' Jesse had seven of his sons pass before Samuel, but Samuel said to him, 'The Lord has not chosen these.' So, he asked Jesse, 'Are these all the sons you have?'" (1 Samuel 16:8-11)

And Jesse remembers, "Oh yeah, that's right; I do have one son who is tending the sheep." And I think implied in that an-swer is, "But I'm sure it's not him; he's just a snot-nosed kid. Per-haps we should have the other seven parade by one more time because maybe you missed something?" But Samuel replies, "Go get him!" So, Jesse sent for him and had him brought in. He was glowing with health, had a fine appearance and handsome features. Then the Lord said, "Rise and anoint him; this is the one" (1 Samuel 16:12).

By the way, Jesse and Samuel are like many of us. They assumed that the future King of Israel had to look a certain way and act a certain way. He had to be a people person. He had to have an impressive resume. He had to have a great education. But God says, "That's not what I'm looking for. That's not what determines a person's usefulness to me. Sure, those other young men are handsome and talented, but they're not right for the job."

This brings up the question, "Why weren't they the right ones?" Well, if we continue to read the story, we discover that God was looking for someone with a specific kind of heart. In other words, even though David was handsome and gifted and talented, that wasn't the criteria that impressed God. God was looking for a person with the right kind of heart.

I see this a lot when I meet individuals who believe they should be on staff at Hope or in the position of an elder. An opportunity for staff advancement or promotion comes up, and someone will say to me, "You know, if I were in that role, I would have more influence." And as I talk to them, I discover that they feel that way because they are gifted with talent and ability. They have a strong background or an impressive resume. From their perspective, they're so much smarter than everyone else. But I don't find anything in the Bible about God using us due to our personal influence.

Paul wrote, "Now it is required that those who have been given a trust must prove faithful" (1 Corinthians 4:2). I'm probably old school, but I think God's desire is that we're faithful wherever He has placed us. If God chooses to give us influence, that's awesome, but He just wants us to be faithful. When you look at the people that God uses in incredible ways, rarely are they the most capable or the most gifted, rarely are they the most talented, rarely are they the smartest, but they're always faithful. In fact, I've discovered in my years of ministry that often the people who have the most talent, ability, education, and experience have a tendency to rely on those things, and like Saul, they crash and burn. And sometimes, they take a whole lot of people down with them. That's why God operates by other criteria. God is simply looking for people who think, "God, I've got nothing without you; I'm totally relying and depending on you."

Before I close this chapter, I want to explain why there is a difference between the things that impress the world and the things that impress God. It's because God's objective is different from the world's objective, and what God wants to accomplish is different from what the world wants to accomplish. In the system in which we live, you and I are basically a means to someone else's end. For example, if you don't do your job at work, you're let go. Your supervisor doesn't say in your annual review, "You haven't sold a thing in seventeen years, but you're such a nice person, we like having you around." The marketplace isn't like that. If you don't perform, you're out. Everyone may love you. Everyone may want to draw your name at Christmas. Everyone may want to hang out with you on the weekend, but if you don't perform, you're out. As a result, there's an element of insecurity in that relationship.

It's also true in some marriages. For some, security in marriage is based on performance and meeting expectations. After thirty-six years of counseling married couples, this is what I've learned: Most people get married for what they hope to gain. "Is it going to make me happy? Is it going to meet my needs? Is it going to complete me? Am I going to be fulfilled?" When we marry someone who has those kinds of high expectations, we often live with a sense of potential failure. There's the fear that no matter what we do, we will not make the grade. And when we don't perform, we feel alienated. Why? That's the nature of performance-oriented relationships—it destroys the relationship by canceling out unconditional love. Therefore, if we can carry our end of the load, we're safe in the relationship. But if we drop our end of the load, guess what happens? Suddenly we are on the outside looking in because our value isn't tied to who we are; our value is tied to how much we do. Jesus addressed this when He was with the disciples. He made the comment: "You know that the rulers of the Gentiles lord it over them, and their high officials exercise authority over them" (Matthew 20:25). It is interesting in this passage that Jesus never says it's wrong, He just states the fact that it's the way it is out there in the world.

But in verse 26, the topic turns to the Kingdom of God and Jesus says to his disciples, "Not so with you." In other words, "That's the way it works in the world, but in here, that's not the way it works," because in God's Kingdom, people are never a means to an end. People *are* the end. In fact, the thing that made Jesus such a radically different leader is that He didn't have an agenda. His followers never felt like they were a means to an end. They never felt used. That's why Jesus could make bold statements as in John 10:10 when He said, "I have come that they may have life, and have it to the full."

But I'm sure the crowd was skeptical when they heard that statement. They probably responded, "Well what else are you trying to do? Because there's got to be more than you just want us to be happy and live this incredible life of fulfillment. There must be some strings attached."

Jesus responded, "Okay, you caught me. There is more because I'm also going to die on the cross for your sins so you can be forgiven and be reconciled and restored back into a relationship with God."

And the crowd again responded, "That's interesting, but what else?"

And Jesus answered, "That's it! I'm just here for you!"

And that's why Jesus could say, "Instead, whoever wants to become great among you must be your servant, and whoever wants to be first must be your slave – just as the Son of Man did not come to be served, but to serve, and to give his life as a ransom for many" (Matthew 20:26-28).

In Jesus' day, that one statement turned the leadership paradigm upside down because even the Son of Man, the one who deserved to be served, didn't have an agenda and didn't come to this earth to be served; He came to serve. The Kingdom of God is built and established on that simple premise. People are the end. And at the end of the day, that's what sets the Kingdom of God apart from the kingdom of man. And that's why God isn't necessarily looking for the talented or the gifted.

Now, if you have talent and gifts, that's great! Use them. After all, God gave them to you. But God is far more interested in how you live the Christian life. I don't know about you, but I have a tendency to avoid people who are constantly reminding me how gifted and talented they are, but when I'm around people who really love people, there's something that draws me. I can't be around that individual without wondering, "Where is it coming from? What is the source of this kind of love?" Understand, that's what gives all of us the incredible potential to be used by God and to do great things in his Kingdom. God is simply looking for those who are willing to love and serve the way He loves and serves. That's it. And when we begin to live this way, our potential for usefulness in God's Kingdom will skyrocket regardless of our gifts and talents.

One of my pet peeves is that we live in a society where our leaders are constantly telling us that we can do anything we want to do and we can be anything we want to be. That's not true! I've been a Dallas Cowboys fan since I was six years old. I would love to have played wide receiver for the Dallas Cowboys. I would love to have been a shooting guard for the Boston Celtics. I would love to have played catcher for the Los Angeles Dodgers, but those dreams are never going to happen. And it's not for lack of desire.

Given the opportunity, I would have tried hard, but I was born neither with the physical aptitude nor the talent it takes to perform at those professional levels. Over the next few pages, as we talk about what it takes to be used in the Kingdom of God, this is what you will discover: It's not about your talents or abilities or education or your family pedigree. It's not about your accomplishments or achievements. It's also not about your past, your history, your failures, or your baggage. We're going to discover that all of us have an equal opportunity to be used by God and to impact those around us.

Chapter 2

Who Knows?

Twenty-five years ago, we were living the dream in the comfort of California. We lived in a beautiful house, drove nice cars, and pastored an established church. My children attended a wonderful Christian school and we enjoyed vacationing in exotic places like Hawaii. Life was good! But then I made the mistake of attending a "Purpose Driven Church Conference." To be honest, I'm not big on church conferences. After being in full-time ministry for an extended period of time, I felt like I'd heard and seen it all. Add that to the fact that I have serious ADHD and a tendency to check out mentally and emotionally. But this conference offered a great excuse to get away for a few days, so I decided to attend.

I don't remember which session, but I remember that it was after lunch and I was struggling to stay alert when Rick Warren made a statement that would change the course of our lives. He said, "Some of you are trying to lead a church that doesn't want to be led. Maybe God wants you to leave that church and start a church that will make a difference for God's Kingdom." From that moment forward, I couldn't shake the idea that God wanted me to uproot my family and relocate to North Carolina for the purpose of starting a new church. Not just any church—a new kind of church—the kind of church where people would feel welcome and accepted . . . where people could find a sense of community and belonging, the kind of church where creativity and relevance would be a part of the DNA. I wanted to start the kind of church that actually makes a difference in the community. But the fears would always creep in and I would think, "It will never work. I'm not a good enough leader. I'm not a good enough teacher. There won't be any money. How am I going to support my family?"

One day, I called a good friend and shared with him all of my fears, concerns, every reason why this move was the wrong move and why it didn't make sense, secretly hoping that he would agree and tell me not to do it. After listening very patiently, he said, "Mike, you're thinking about it the wrong way. You need to be asking, 'God, what could you do through me and Laura if we were 100% willing and available?' That's the way you should be thinking because who knows what God may do if you're willing to trust him."

And so, we began to pray and think in a different way. Now, I'm not going to lie to you, even after my friend's pep talk, the fears continued, but God kept reminding me of my friend's words, "Who knows? This kind of church might work. Who knows? God may be gracious and strong and surprise everybody."

As I look back at the times in my life when God prompted me to do something, more often than not, my natural focus was on the worst-case scenario. But time and time again, the Spirit of God would come alongside me and say, "But what if it's the best-case scenario?" When He prompted me to start Hope Community Church, I listened and obeyed. I can't imagine my life today if I'd given in to my fears and not made myself available to God. I'm glad I decided that this is how I want to live my life.

Just like any pastor, the part of my job I dread the most is reading emails. Either the music is too loud or the lights are moving around too much or the message isn't deep enough or the message is too deep. At the same time, one of the highlights of my job is reading emails. For example, on my sixtieth birthday, I received an email—my best birthday present that year.

A young college student who attends Hope wrote:

I came from a very dysfunctional family. My dad died when I was seven years old of a cocaine overdose and my mom was addicted to pain pills. I have a twin sister who is my rock. We finished our high school careers with state records and national times in track and field and we committed to Indiana University. However, things changed quickly.

Our grandparents were our caregivers and our biggest supporters, but my grandmother was diagnosed with pancreatic cancer in August 2014 and passed away eight weeks later. This led to depression and anxiety for the first time in my life and I continued to not understand how God would let this happen to me and my family. After all, I had already been through a lot.

Shortly after that, I was injured, yet continued to remain in a toxic and emotionally abusing team atmosphere. Finally, I decided it was time for much-needed change. I left Indiana for the first time ever and moved eleven hours away from my twin sister to become independent, another first in my life. And that's when God placed amazing coaches at North Carolina State in my life, which led to me being introduced to Hope Community Church.

This past February, after I finished a long run in Raleigh, I came home to discover many missed calls from my uncle. My grandfather had passed away from a heart attack. Other than my twin sister, I had lost the two most important people in my life in a span of 1-1/2 years. Throughout all this I continued to struggle deeply with the grieving process and the pain of having to do life without them. I realized how much my faith had faded, but I felt something when I attended Hope Community Church. I continued, week after week, challenged to dig deeper into my faith. I had considered myself a Christian since middle school, but had never really done much to grow. Your "Joy" sermon inspired me to continue to find faith in the God who brings purpose to our pain. So, thank you for inspiring me to dig deeper to find joy and happiness through God's goodness and remem-

ber my faith through trials and struggles. I finally realize that there's more to life than running around an oval and my worth is more than the race I run. You inspired me to be the best person I can be. I continue to pray that you find happiness and joy through your current struggles. Happy Birthday!

Tears streamed down my face as I read that email. As I stated earlier when you realize that God somehow worked through you to impact someone's life, well, it's a thrill that never goes away.

In the previous chapter, we talked about God's criteria for usefulness and what God is looking for in a person. We learned that his criteria are very different from the things we, as worldly people, often think. God does not look at appearances; He looks for an available and willing heart. If we are ever going to be used by God in ways that we never dreamed or imagined, we must understand that key point.

However, if we're honest, we keep evaluating ourselves by the external, so we assume there's no way that God could ever use us. For example, "There's no way . . . my family background is too dysfunctional." However, if we read the Bible, coming from a dysfunctional family doesn't seem to be a disqualification. Solomon's mom was Bathsheba, the woman who committed adultery with David. Consequently, Solomon was the result of an adulterous affair, yet he overcame his family history to become, according to the Bible, the wisest man who ever lived.

How about Joseph? He was the favorite son of Jacob and the recipient of that beautiful coat of many colors. Eventually, the eleven brothers had all they could stand of Daddy's little pet. They were so over Joseph's special multicolored coat and the preferential treatment he received. One day, Joseph went out to visit his brothers while they were working in the field—Joseph didn't do that kind of work, after all, he was daddy's favorite. His brothers were tired of him and decided, "That's it; we're done!" They sold Joseph into slavery and told their parents that Joseph had been killed by a wild animal. How's that for a dysfunctional family? However, through a series of circumstances, Joseph became the prime minister of Egypt, the second most powerful position in the most powerful country at that time, and God used Joseph to save the Hebrew people from starvation.

Ever read the story of Ruth? Ruth was the original Bachelorette without the trashy morals. Through a series of amazing circumstances, she falls in love with a rich man named Boaz. The story of Ruth and Boaz is beautiful, and I love what it says in Ruth 4:13, "So Boaz took Ruth and she became his wife. When he made love to her, the Lord enabled her to conceive, and she gave birth to a son."

Ruth named him Obed. Obed grew up and had a son named Jesse. Jesse grew up and had a son named David. Through David came the Messiah, Jesus.

Now let's go back to the story of Ruth and Boaz. Do you know who Boaz's mom was? She was a woman named Rahab — Rahab the Hooker, Rahab the Harlot, Rahab the Prostitute. She was the one who hid the Hebrew spies in the city of Jericho before the walls came down. My point is, Rahab the Harlot is in the lineage of Jesus. Yes, she is in the family tree of Jesus. I like to tell my congregation, Rahab put the "Ho, ho, ho" in Christmas!

There's another guy named Judah who had sex with his daughter-in-law. He's also in the family tree of Jesus.

You can't make this stuff up! It is as if God was making the statement, "I don't care about your family background, I can use you."

Another excuse we make is, "God can't use me because I'm not smart enough." Well, the Bible isn't about the smartest people who ever lived. Don't get me wrong, some of the people in the Bible were brilliant, some were average, and some of them were below average. In fact, the Twelve Disciples were basically ignorant, uneducated men.

Robert Coleman addresses this in his small, but powerful book, *Master Plan of Evangelism*:

> *What is revealing about these men is that at first, they do not impress us as being key men. None of them occupied prominent places in the Synagogue, nor did any of them belong to the Levitical priesthood. For the most part, they were common laboring men, probably having no professional training beyond the rudiments of knowledge necessary for their vocation. Perhaps a few of them came from families of some considerable means, such as the sons of Zebedee but none of them could have been considered wealthy. They had no academic degrees in the arts and philosophies of their day. Like their Master, their formal education likely consisted only of the Synagogue schools. Most of them were raised in the poor section of the country around Galilee. Apparently, the only one of the twelve who came from the more refined region of Judea was Judas Iscariot. By any standard of sophisticated culture then and now they would surely be considered as a rather ragged aggregation of souls. One might wonder how Jesus could ever use them. They were impulsive, temperamental, easily offended, and had all the prejudices of their environment. In short, these men selected by the Lord to be His assistants represented an average cross section of the lot of society in their day. Not the kind of group one would expect to win the world for Christ.* (22-23)

Maybe you have the idea that when Jesus was putting together his Twelve Disciples, He went around Judea and visited the synagogues and the seminaries to pick out the cream of the crop. That's not the case. He chose ordinary, garden-variety men with a basic knowledge of life. He picked people like you and me; they were the ones He called. My point is, intellect or lack of, isn't a big deal to God. Now, you may never become captain of a nuclear submarine, win a Pulitzer Prize, discover the cure for cancer, or work for NASA, but intelligence is not the qualifier to do great things in the Kingdom of God.

Another excuse is, "God can't use me because of my past. If people knew my past they would never take me seriously." There's one thing you should know: God only uses sinners. If you're a sinner, it means you meet the required qualification. You're exactly who God is looking for. If you don't believe that, think about the people whom Jesus called.

Matthew was a tax collector who stole money from his own people, the Jews, and he did it on behalf of Rome, so he could live a lavish lifestyle. The Jews absolutely hated Matthew. He was considered a traitor to his own people; yet, God allowed Matthew to write a book of the Bible. Some of you even name your sons after Matthew.

What about the Apostle Paul? You think you've been bad? Read the Book of Acts and you will discover that before Paul became a follower of Jesus, he went around burning down churches and arresting Jesus' followers. Acts 9 tells us that he held their coats while Christians were being stoned to death. But God thinks, "That's not a big deal to me. You can't believe what we're going to do together."

And Peter? He denied knowing Jesus three times when Jesus needed him the most. Within a few weeks of his denial, he's standing on some street corner in downtown Jerusalem telling people about Jesus' death, burial, and resurrection. According to Acts 2, three thousand people converted from Judaism to following Jesus that very day, and that was the beginning of the Christian Church.

As I said earlier, God has brought some individuals to Hope with pretty colorful pasts. For example, Becky was employed as an exotic dancer and living with a drug dealer who wasn't her husband when she stumbled into Hope for an Easter service. On that first visit to Hope, she accepted Christ. The next week, she applied for the receptionist job at the church. We hired her, loved on her, and mentored her in her faith. Over the years, she has shared her story with wayward girls and God has used her to reach others with the Gospel.

At this point, you might be thankful that God hasn't led you to be a part of Hope Community Church. But if Becky's story sounds a little like your story—maybe you weren't an exotic dancer, but you would definitely put yourself in the category of an "All-Pro" sinner—and because of that you wonder, how could God use me? Then this is what I want you to understand: Your past is not a deal-breaker for God. In fact, your past may be the very thing that He uses to impact others.

What we think is so important often isn't important to God. Things we think are deal breakers aren't deal breakers for God. Remember, God is looking for people who have a simple willingness to love and serve the way Jesus loved and served, but He's also looking for a *pure* heart. David wrote, "Who may ascend the mountain of the Lord? Who may stand in his holy place? The one who has clean hands and a pure heart, who does not trust in an idol or swear by a false god" (Psalm 24:3-4).

What does that mean? Well, it doesn't mean that God is looking for people with a perfect or sinless heart. A pure heart means an unmixed heart. In other words, our objectives, agenda, passion, and purpose for our life lines up with God's objectives, agenda, passion, and purpose for our life. It means we are more interested in God's will and plan than our own. We trust in God. That's a pure heart.

You can see this in 1 Samuel 13. Initially, the people of Israel asked for God's help in finding a king. Samuel reassured them that God would help them but if they turn away from God and disobey Him, they and their king, Saul, would perish. Even with Samuel's warnings, Saul behaved like a fool and followed his own heart. So, Samuel tells Saul, "That's it; you disobeyed God. You did a foolish thing by not carrying out the command He gave you. As a result, you can't be king anymore."

Saul's problem wasn't his lack of gifts; Saul's problem was that he was incredibly gifted. In fact, he was so gifted and talented, it was pretty much impossible for him to be humble. And he found himself relying on his gifts and his talents and his position as king instead of depending on God. Even though he had everything he needed, humanly speaking, to be a great king, he blew it. In other words, Saul trusted in his own abilities instead of trusting in God. He became his own idol. He had a mixed heart and it wasn't in alignment with God's heart. And God began to search for a person after His own heart.

God hasn't changed his criteria for usefulness in his kingdom. He is still looking for men and women who are willing to say, "God, here I am; whatever you need or however you want to use me or wherever you want to use me, I am in it for you."

It's not about being capable; it's about having a pure, unmixed heart. We're all capable. God has given each of us some kind of ability and talent. The problem is that our hearts do not always align with God's heart.

I think that a lot of our struggle, especially in America, is that we've bought into the American Dream. We want the perfect career, the perfect house, the perfect car, the perfect kids, and we want it now. We want a wrinkle-free Heaven, now! That's the American Dream. And so, we make a plan and we work the plan to accomplish that goal. The problem with that kind of thinking is that God may have a plan for us that doesn't include the American Dream, but that doesn't stop us from pursuing it, does it? And so, we end up with our own agenda. As a result, our heart is tainted. We have one foot in the world because we want what we want, and we have one foot in the Kingdom of God because we need God to help our dream become a reality. Plus, we want to make sure that we get into heaven when we die. We're torn. We don't have an unmixed heart; we have a mixed heart, yet when we meet someone with a pure, unmixed heart, it's so unusual that it has an impact on us.

A few weeks ago, as I arrived at the church. There was a gentleman I didn't recognize sitting outside our church offices. I asked if had he had been helped, and he said, "Yes, I have an appointment with one of the pastors at nine o'clock."

He looked up at me and said, "I recognize you. I've been watching you online." He started crying.

Now, I may not be the most sensitive guy in the world, but even I knew that something was wrong. So, I grabbed him, pulled him into an office, and said, "Listen, I've got a meeting in a few minutes, but it can wait. What's going on?"

He told me his story. He was a corporate lawyer from another state living the American Dream until the day his wife informed him that she was leaving him for another man. She took their daughters and moved to North Carolina. He was left, alone and miserable; his life had fallen apart. He realized that he needed to relocate to North Carolina. He left his job and moved hundreds of miles to be near his children, but he hadn't been able to find a new job in the area. He thought maybe we could help. So, he walked in hoping to meet with a pastor who could speak wisdom into his life, but instead, he ended up with me. I did pray with him, and I tried to encourage him with all the clichés that pastors are taught to say during tough and trying times. When I finished, I asked, "What can I do for you right now?"

He said he had to find a job and asked for any information or anyone with whom he could network. Immediately, I thought of Scott, who is, without a doubt, one of the most gifted, competent individuals I have ever met. For example, after completing his undergraduate degree, Scott went on to Harvard Business School. While a student at Harvard, he started a company which he sold for millions of dollars a few years later, and eventually relocated to North Carolina where he became an elder at our church. Scott is one of those people that God has blessed with the amazing ability and bandwidth to accomplish what a lot of us can only imagine. I knew immediately that Scott would be the perfect person to help this man. And so, I gave him Scott's number and told him it may take a week or two to connect because Scott could be anywhere in the world.

When our meeting concluded, I called Scott. The call went straight to voicemail, so I left a message explaining the situation and then asked Scott if he could carve out a few minutes to talk to this man. Five minutes later, Scott was texting me and telling me that he already set up a lunch appointment for that very day! My point is, as busy and as capable as Scott is, he realizes that, at the end of the day, what God has called us to do is not to build businesses and sit on boards; God has called us to love and serve because the end is people, not an organization, not a business, not even a church. People aren't a means to an end; people *are* the end.

So, when God says, "Here's your assignment. Here's how I want to use you, this is who I want you to reach and impact," watch out! He will wear you out and it will be the joy of a lifetime.

Now, you may be thinking, "I'm not sure I have a pure heart. I've got one foot in the world and one foot in the Kingdom." I get that. It's hard to commit everything you have and are to God, so maybe you're not there yet. But does that mean that you shouldn't be involved in loving and serving others until you have a pure heart? No. However, the purity of the heart will determine the extent to which God is able to use us. God never said we have to be perfect before He can use us, and once we are willing to serve, God will begin to change and purify our hearts until our motives and our purpose for life begin to line up with His.

So, the takeaway from this chapter should be, "Okay, God, here I go; I'm willing to walk down this road with you. And in the process of us walking together, purify my heart. Create in me an unmixed heart. Teach me to want what you want more than what I want." I promise you, that response is far more important to God than anything else. And don't waste energy worrying about how to do what God asks. As we're going to see in the next chapter, God already knows how to do whatever it is that needs to be done. God is looking for someone whose heart aligns with His. And when you commit to allow God to purify your heart, God may take the very thing that you feel defines you, and use it for His purpose and glory.

One of my favorite scenes in the Bible is in Exodus. After Moses killed the Egyptian in Exodus 2, he fled to Midian to hide out in the desert. In Exodus 3, Moses has been in the wilderness for forty years. While there, he's been working for his father-in-law, Jethro. That means that Moses went from living in Pharaoh's palace to this dead-end job on the backside of the Sinai Desert. He spent every day doing the same thing—watching sheep. It was hot, dry, and miserable. And I'm sure he was sick and tired of the desert, but in Exodus 3, everything starts to change:

> "Now Moses was tending the flock of Jethro his father-in-law, the priest of Midian, and he led the flock to the far side of the wilderness and came to Horeb, the mountain of God. There the angel of the Lord appeared to him in flames of fire from within a bush. Moses saw that though the bush was on fire it did not burn up. So, Moses thought, 'I will go over and see this strange sight—why the bush does not burn up.' When the Lord saw that he had gone over to look, God called to him from within the bush, 'Moses! Moses!' And Moses said, 'Here I am.'"
> (Exodus 3:1-4)

If you continue reading, you'll discover that God said to Moses, "I am choosing you to deliver my people from slavery." By Exodus 4, there's a showdown between God and Moses.

Moses has every excuse in the world why God could never use him to be the deliverer. Finally, God asks Moses a question in Exodus 4:2: "What is that in your hand?"

And Moses responded, "God, you know what I have in my hand—it's a staff." But it was much more than a staff. Moses used it for protection to keep wild animals at bay. He used it to negotiate difficult terrain and to lean on when he was tired. For Moses, the staff was his connection to life. It was his identity! It defined who he was.

But God says to Moses, "Throw it on the ground." And according to Exodus 4:3, "Moses threw it on the ground and it became a snake, and he ran from it." Moses did what any intelligent person would do as that snake started slithering around on the ground—he ran! God said to Moses in verse 4, "Reach out your hand and take it by the tail."

I'm sure that Moses was thinking, "Are you serious—pick it up by the tail? Everyone knows you never pick a snake up by its tail!"

But God persisted, "Pick it up by the tail, Moses."

So, Moses picks up the snake by the tail, and it becomes a shepherd's staff. But it's not an ordinary staff anymore—something has happened, something has changed. According to the last part of Exodus 4:20, when Moses obeyed God and threw it down and picked it back up, it became the staff of God. Moses used God's staff to part the Red Sea. He used God's staff to bring water out of the rock. He used God's staff to win battles. In other words, the very thing that Moses was reluctant to release was the very thing that God used in his life.

Here's my question for you: What's preventing you from doing what God is calling you to do? What excuses are you hiding behind? Is it a lack of education? A successful career? A relationship? A Dysfunctional past? Or is it the pursuit of your own dreams and plans? Whatever it is, God will not give in or give up. His challenge to us is no different than his challenge to

Moses, "Throw it down!" And when you throw down whatever it is that's keeping you from being willing, the thing you throw down and surrender is often the very thing that God will have you pick back up and use for His purpose and glory. The questions are: Do you have a pure, unmixed heart? Are you ready and willing to do what God has designed specifically for you?

Chapter 3
Focus on the "Who," not the "How"

We've all seen enough movies to know that there are certain essential components if the story is going to be epic. First, there's an important mission—an ark to be dug up, a Holy Grail to be found, a pretty girl to be rescued, a city to be protected. Second, some form of opposition must be overcome—a villain, an enemy, a traitor—an epic has to have that formidable opponent to provide conflict. Third, a carefully thought-out strategy that holds the highest probability of achieving the goal must at least be on the drawing board if not directly employed. Finally, there's a main character or hero/heroine with his or her own signature style such as James Bond or Wonder Woman.

The Bible is full of epic dramas. There's Moses with his people standing at the Red Sea with nowhere to go as the Egyptian army bears down upon them. There's Abraham holding a dagger high in the air, ready to plunge it into Isaac's chest, hoping for a miracle. There's Daniel in a den surviving a night among the hungry lions. Probably one of the most familiar and most loved is the story of David and Goliath. Without a doubt, it provides all of the elements of the epic drama.

In case you're not that familiar with the story, the initial tension is two great opposing armies preparing for battle: The Army of Israel, the "good guys," against the Philistines, the "bad guys." The Philistines were from the country of Philistia, located near the Mediterranean Sea, very close to some key Israeli cities like Bethlehem and Jerusalem. In fact, there are only about thirty miles separating Philistia and Jerusalem. Not only was Philistia strategically located to be a constant pain in the backside of the Hebrew people because of the proximity, the Philistines were constantly trying to gain ground and take land away from Israel.

With all of the elements in place to make this an epic, let's pick up the story in 1 Samuel 17:1-2. "Now the Philistines gathered their forces for war and assembled at Sokoh in Judah. They pitched camp at Ephes Dammim, between Sokoh and Azekah. Saul and the Israelites assembled and camped in the Valley of Elah and drew up their battle line to meet the Philistines." (I recently took some people to Israel, and we stood in the Valley of Elah. The valley is less than a mile wide with hills situated on each side. I could picture the Philistines occupying one hill and the Israelites occupying the other with the valley between them.)

And now we meet the villain; his name is Goliath. Goliath was from the city of Gath, located in Philistia. He was six cubits and a span, which means nothing to us, but translates to about 9-1/2 to 10 feet tall. According to 1 Samuel 17:5-7: "He had a bronze helmet on his head and wore a coat of scale armor of bronze weighing five thousand shekels; on his legs he wore bronze greaves, and a bronze javelin was slung on his back. His spear shaft was like a weaver's rod, and its iron point weighed six hundred shekels. His shield bearer went ahead of him." His bronze helmet on his head and scale armor of bronze weighed 5000 shekels. That's 175 pounds. Understand that this is a bad dude.

According to the story, this giant of a man would walk out into the Valley of Elah every day to taunt the Army of Israel by suggesting a representative battle. A representative battle was suggested when there was a small issue like a border dispute to settle. It was a pretty smart idea. Instead of a lot of soldiers dying, a warrior would be chosen from each side, and they would go "mano a mano." The Philistines believed that it was the gods of each nation fighting through these two men, so actually, the gods would settle the dispute. I'm assuming this was a much bigger dispute because for forty days, Goliath would put his armor on, walk out to the Valley, stand in the middle, and according to 1 Samuel 17:8-9, shout to the ranks of Israel, "Why do you come out and line up for battle? Am I not a Philistine, and are you not the servants of Saul? Choose a man and have him come down to me. If he is able to fight and kill me, we will become your subjects; but if I overcome him and kill him, you will become our subjects and serve us."

Back at the ranch, David is taking care of his father's sheep while his three older brothers were serving in the Israelite army. One day, David's father, Jesse, called David in from the field and said, "Listen, this is what I want you to do. I've put together a little care package and I want you to go down to the battlefront and deliver the package. I also want you to check on your brothers and see how they're holding up." David does exactly as he is told.

However, when David arrives at the battlefront, he's confused by what he witnesses. While he's catching up with his brothers, Goliath comes out and goes through his daily routine. And as he talks smack about the God of Israel, David watches the Hebrew soldiers run and hide, and he's shocked that no one is willing to take on Goliath. So, David asked a soldier standing nearby, "What's the reward for taking out this big blowhard?"

The soldier responds, "Wealth, tax cuts, and the opportunity to marry the king's daughter!"

When the news reached King Saul that David was inquiring about facing Goliath, Saul said, "Bring this David to me."

Now, before we move forward, let's put some things in perspective. David is probably a young teen, yet before King Saul and his military commanders, he says, "Don't worry; I'll fight the giant." I'm sure that David's confidence was met with some nervous laughter.

Saul responds, "You're just a kid—you are way over your head."

David then takes this opportunity to share his resume with King Saul:

> "Your servant has been keeping his father's sheep. When a lion or a bear came and carried off a sheep from the flock, I went after it, struck it and rescued the sheep from its mouth. When it turned on me, I seized it by its hair, struck it, and killed it. Your servant has killed the lion and the bear; this uncircumcised Philistine will be like one of them because he has defied the armies of the living God. The Lord who rescued me from the paw of the lion and the paw of the bear will rescue me from the hand of this Philistine." (1 Samuel 17: 34-37)

Say what you want, but the kid had a confidence level off the charts.

By the way, do you know what the problem was for Saul and his troops? The problem was that they were convinced their potential for victory over Goliath hinged on who they were, what they could do, and the skills they had developed as soldiers over the years. In other words, they were depending on all the things that an army of soldiers would rely on. They had been standing on that hill every day looking out on the valley, comparing themselves to Goliath, and thinking, "He's so big; he's so mean; he's so brave! We're so short; we're so nice; we're so scared. There is no possible way we can defeat him." In other words, they were focused on the external—Goliath's size, ability, and strength. They were focused on what he could do versus what they could do. Their biggest mistake was that they forgot to factor God into the equation.

From their perspective, the story was about the Philistine army, with their superstar named Goliath, taking on the Army of Israel that was void of any superstar, whatsoever. That's why King Saul was trying to bribe any and all takers with incentives like his daughter's hand in marriage. Saul tells them he'll also throw in wealth and a lifetime exemption from paying taxes! Even with all that, there were still no takers. Why? Well, it was because they were asking the wrong question; they were asking, "How?" And no one could come up with the right answer.

In the meantime, while the Philistines were having the time of their lives taunting the Israelite army and their God, David shows up with his picnic basket full of goodies for his brothers and he asks the right question in 1 Samuel 17:26; "Who is this uncircumcised Philistine that defies the God of the Army of Israel?" You see, from David's perspective, Goliath wasn't their problem. Goliath was God's problem, and Goliath was no problem for God.

Was Goliath a problem for the Army of Israel? Yes! Was Goliath a problem for David? Yes! Would Goliath be a problem for you and me? Yes! Was Goliath a problem for God? No!

David introduces an entirely different perspective into the equation. David sees this situation as a showdown between Goliath's strength and God's strength. In other words, David did what, as Christians, we so often fail to do: He factored God into the equation. And what seemed like an obstacle from a human perspective became an opportunity for God to demonstrate His power.

This is a great lesson for all of us. Do you know the kind of person that God uses? He uses men and women who see obstacles as opportunities.

David knew what everybody else was overlooking. David knew that he worshipped and served a God that created the universe out of nothing. Nothing was too difficult for God. He understood that the "how" is no problem for God. God just needed someone to be the "who."

In my personal experience, whenever God nudges me to do something, He doesn't show me the "how" until I commit to being the "who." Starting Hope Community Church is one of the best illustrations of that process.

When we moved from the San Francisco area to Cary, North Carolina, we started the church in a school. Eventually, the school was to be remodeled and we were kicked to the curb with nowhere to go. I was still working construction at the time, so I didn't have a lot of spare time to look for a new facility. To make matters worse, Cary was a rapidly growing area—it seemed like every school already had a church meeting in its facility, and in some cases, there were two churches meeting on the same campus. The only lead for the possibility of weekend services was a funeral home. Laura let me know that if we met in a funeral home, she would be attending another church. So, I gave her the task of finding us a new place to meet. She contacted a realtor who had a listing for a commercial building. It was divided into three parts with an office supply store in one section and a dressmaker in the other. Ironically, the third section had been used by a church, but it was a mess. The rent for that portion was $3000 a month, which was quite a jump from the $600 we had been paying at the school. However, the owner of the building was a Christian, and the agreement was that all of the rent would go towards a down-payment on the building if we were able to purchase it at some point.

The leaders met in the building to see it and pray, and we took up an offering to upfit it. We needed $12,000 to purchase chairs, a sound system, and supplies. As we passed around a cardboard box that night we collected $14,000. Over the next two weeks, we cleaned and painted and worked tirelessly to set up church in that dreary little building. We had no idea how we were going to make it, but God did.

We now lovingly look back on those years as the "firetrap" years, but it was during those years that God began to bless us and we started to grow. We eventually knocked out some walls and enlarged the auditorium to accommodate a capacity of five hundred. Before long, one service filled up and we started a second . . . and then a third. Then Saturday services. We were able to purchase the entire building and grow our family ministries. We were out of parking and the price of land was going up around us; no matter how much we grew, we could never seem to get ahead of the curve. We decided to do what every church does when it's facing a Red Sea with no options in sight: We decided to pray. We held a twenty-four-hour prayer vigil. During that twenty-four hours of prayer, someone who showed up to pray and shared that a businessman in the community was interested in giving away a piece of property to a church of his choice. He had been looking for a church to inhabit that property for over fifteen years, so my hopes weren't too high. But after meeting the infamous Mr. David Martin, I learned that he only wanted to make sure that the church would reach the surrounding community with the Gospel. He didn't want to give it to a church that wasn't concerned about impacting those around them.

After a year of talking, courting, and praying, a simple handshake sealed the deal. He gave the property to our church! But the obstacles didn't stop there. The plans to build a church and school on the property were submitted to the city and were unanimously rejected. Wow! After all of that prayer and time and generosity, our dream was shattered. But God had other plans. We met on the property and prayed for a change of heart. When the city met the next month and revisited the proposal, they voted unanimously in favor of the building. Proverbs 21:1 says, "In the Lord's hand the king's heart is a stream of water that he channels toward all who please him."

But even that miracle didn't solve all our problems. There were many nights where I tossed and turned in bed wondering how we were going to build the building. It was great to have free property, but we didn't have the money to build, and if we did, how were we going to pay the bills to keep it running?

But, it was as if God said, "Listen, I've got the 'how' figured out, I just need the 'who,'" So, we stepped out on faith and sold the firetrap and moved temporarily into a school with more capacity. In the two-year period, it took to build our new building, we grew from a congregation of a thousand to a congregation of over three thousand. When we walked into our new facility, we walked in with the financial base to use it for God's glory.

God already had the "how" figured out; He was just looking for the "who."

It works the same way in our personal lives. God nudges us. We feel something in our heart, but all we can see is the obstacle. However, if we take that first step, God turns those obstacles into opportunities. In those areas where we are the weakest, that's where God will show up and bring glory to Himself. When we are the weakest, He is the strongest. You can't, but God can.

By the way, the story of David and Goliath would have been entirely different if another soldier had stepped up and fought Goliath. It could have been about some guy hiding behind a tree thinking, "You know, I'm not the brightest bulb in the box and my future isn't looking all that great; maybe this is my big break—marrying into the king's family, given half the wealth of the kingdom, never paying taxes for the rest of my life. It's a pretty sweet deal. Who knows, maybe Goliath will charge in all jacked up on adrenaline, he'll over-swing, and lose his balance; I'll kick him in the knee and he'll go down! Then I'll cut his ugly head off and be a hero!"

If the story had gone down that way, everybody would've said, "Lucky dude had a good day." But it wasn't just *any* soldier. David had nothing going on externally that made him look like a good candidate for this task, but God said, "I'll take those odds! Send in the shepherd, sit back, and watch what I do through him!" And so, David made his way out into the middle of the Valley, no worries whatsoever. From David's perspective, Goliath, the obstacle, was nothing more than an opportunity for God to show up and be God. He had a slingshot and he knew what to do with it; he trusted God to do the other 95%. And, sure enough, God came through in a powerful way.

In the very same way, your potential in God's kingdom depends on your willingness to see the obstacles that you're facing as opportunities for God to show up and do something unique and powerful in your life. In other words, when God places a burden on your heart to reach someone, to get involved with a ministry, to make a financial gift, or to get involved with a project, that is your cue to move. He wants you to do what you know how to do while trusting God to do what only He can do. It is not your job to get hung up on the "how;" it is not your job to wait until you have all your questions answered beforehand. Once God places that burden on your heart and you know what He wants you to do, don't let the "how" become an obstacle. Let me give you some steps that will help you begin to apply this:

Step 1: Identify the obstacles in your life.

I can promise you this: If you are a follower of Jesus Christ, there is something that God wants you to do because God's desire is to bring His Kingdom to this earth. According to 2 Peter 3:9, it's God's desire that no one perishes and that everyone comes to repentance. You are part of His plan to accomplish this. On the other hand, you may be doing your best to ignore God because you're focused on all the reasons why you're not the right person for the task. When God begins to move in your life, you need to identify the obstacle that is preventing you from doing what God is asking. In fact, if your attitude is, "God, I want you to use me, but . . ." How you finish that sentence is your obstacle.

For some of you, that unfinished sentence represents a fear, and that fear is keeping you from being the "who." I'll let you in on a secret: God loves to use scared people. In fact, sometimes He only uses scared people. Moses was scared to death to go back to Egypt and face Pharaoh. Gideon was scared to death to be the captain of the army. Jonah was scared to death to go to Nineveh. So, if you're scared to death to do what God is asking, you're the perfect candidate to do it!

For others, that unfinished sentence represents your reputation. Maybe there's somebody in your life with whom you attend school or work, and you would love nothing more than to reach them with the life-changing message of the Gospel. However, you spent so many years partying your brains out with that person before you became a Christian, you assume that they will never ever take you seriously; yet, the entire Bible is proof that God loves people with bad reputations.

Step 2: See your obstacles as opportunities.

Maybe your obstacle is a dysfunctional background, an addiction, a temptation. Maybe it is fear or your past reputation. You need to constantly remind yourself that your obstacle is actually an opportunity. And it is never a limitation for God.

Step 3: Be willing to be the "who" and trust God to show you the "how."

Begin to believe, "I can't, but He can." You have to get to the place of total reliance on God. Accept the reality that you have no idea how to do what God wants you to do. David had no idea how God was going to do what needed to be done. But David thought, "I have a slingshot, and I know how to use it; let's start there."

I'm telling you, when you rely on God, He is going to use you. And it's probably not going to play out in your mind the way you think. God will take your life and use you in a way that will absolutely surprise you.

By the way, according to historians and archaeologists, based on Goliath's armor, David had little to no chance of sinking that shot. There was maybe a two to three square inch area on Goliath's helmet where he was vulnerable. Best-case scenario:

David puts out an eye, maybe breaks a bone. But most likely, the stone harmlessly bounces off of Goliath's helmet. The odds of making the perfect shot were slim to none.

Do you know why I point that out? Do you know how much room God needs to use you to do something great for him? Do you know how much of a chance He needs? Not much at all; slim to none. In fact, I think God loves those kinds of odds. He wants you to say, "I don't have the strength. I don't have the talent. I don't have the money. But, God the battle is yours and I'm going to be the 'who' and trust."

One of my favorite verses in the Bible is 1 Corinthians 1:27. It says, "But God chose the foolish things of the world to shame the wise; God chose the weak things of the world to shame the strong." If they put pictures in the Bible the way they sometimes do in dictionaries, my picture would be right there next to this verse.

What is it God is moving you to do? Who is He wanting you to reach? You don't need to know "how" but you need to be willing to be the "who." When you make that decision, buckle up! You're in for the ride of your life. When God gets a hold of someone who's willing to be the "who," there's absolutely nothing that He cannot accomplish with that person.

Chapter 4
You've Got to See the Big Picture

We all know that our God is big and powerful, yet we don't think about Him that way on a daily basis. We don't wake every morning and ask, "God, what do you want to do through me today? Who do you want me to reach? How can you use me?"

Part of the challenge is the inability to see the big picture. But in this chapter, you're going to see that God is looking for people with an eternal perspective who can look beyond this life and are willing to make the necessary adjustments considering what they know about the future. By the way, it's hard for us to have an eternal perspective because we only get sixty, seventy, eighty, ninety, maybe a hundred years here on planet earth. And no matter how long our life may be, it never seems to be enough because it goes by so quickly. James 4:14 says, "What is your life? You are a mist that appears for a little while and then vanishes." And since that is true, we try to pack in everything we can between the bookends of life because we think that when it's over, it's over. But as Christians, we know that's not true. We know that, according to the Bible, this life is really nothing more than the warm-up act for all eternity. And what we do with the few years God gives on planet earth will determine how we spend our entire eternity. We *know* that; we just don't *live* like we know that.

Jesus talked about this in the Parable of the Mina in Luke 19. What's interesting is that this comes right on the heels of Jesus' encounter with Zacchaeus. Remember Zacchaeus? Zacchaeus was the "wee little man and the wee little man was he." But Za-

cchaeus was more than a wee little man; he was also a tax collector, which meant he was a Jew taking taxes from the Jews and
giving them to Rome. And, of course, in the process, he took
some money off the top for himself so that he could live a very
lavish life. Understand, from a Jewish perspective, Zacchaeus
was a traitor and a sellout. Well, one day Zacchaeus heard
through the grapevine that Jesus was coming through town so
he "climbed up in the Sycamore tree, for the Lord he wanted to
see. Yet, as the Savior passed that way, He looked up in the tree.
And He said, 'Zacchaeus, you come down from there, for I'm
going to your house today.'"

It was scandalous in Jesus' day for him to go to this man's
home. Even the crowds were wondering what was going on.
We're not told what exactly happened in that house, but when
Zacchaeus emerged after his one-on-one time with Jesus, he
made this bold statement in Luke 19:8: "Look, Lord! Here and
now I give half of my possessions to the poor, and if I have
cheated anybody out of anything, I will pay back four times the
amount."

Then Jesus made a statement: "Today salvation has come to
this house, because this man, too, is a son of Abraham. For the
Son of Man came to seek and to save the lost." (Luke 19:9-10)

By the way, when Jesus made statements like, "Today salvation has come," the crowds became very excited because they
thought He was getting ready to establish His Kingdom on
earth. Keep in mind, most of the people that followed Jesus at
this point in his ministry were following him not because they
thought He was the Messiah, but because they expected him to
establish an earthly kingdom and they wanted to make sure that
they were going to be a part of it. In other words, they were waiting for him to overthrow the Romans and take the throne as
King of Israel. From their perspective, forget eternity, it was
about the here and now. They were focused on this world and
on this life. But Jesus knew that for them to be able to make the

impact that He needed them to make once He was gone, they were going to have to learn to measure their lives in light of eternity. Jesus knew He was a few days from crucifixion and He would be buried in a borrowed tomb; three days later, He would rise from the dead, spend a few weeks with his followers, then ascend to heaven. He also knew that when He left this earth, He was going to give his followers the responsibility of spreading the Gospel throughout the world. If his followers were going to succeed, these men had to be able to live their lives and make decisions considering eternity, not the here and now. They had to be able to see the big picture. If not, Jesus knew that the mission of establishing His church would be short-lived. He needed His followers to understand that the end of this life isn't really the end of this life. It is the beginning. And to make sure that His followers understood this truth, Jesus told them the parable of the minas in Luke 19:12-15. He said:

> "A man of noble birth went to a distant country to have himself appointed king and then to return. So he called ten of his servants and gave them ten minas. 'Put this money to work,' he said, 'until I come back.' But his subjects hated him and sent a delegation after him to say, 'We don't want this man to be our king.' He was made king, however, and returned home. Then he sent for the servants to whom he had given the money, in order to find out what they had gained with it."

In order to understand this parable, there are five specific elements to identify. First, there's a "man of noble birth." The man of noble birth represents Jesus who will soon leave earth for the distant country of heaven. But after a period of time, though we're not told how long, he will return to earth to establish his authority. Second, there's a group of servants, and these servants represent people like you and me. In fact, they represent all be-

lievers between the time Christ leaves earth and returns again.
Third, there's an amount of money that's discussed. It's called a
mina and it represented about a hundred days' worth of wages.
So, the nobleman gave each servant one-third of what he would
typically earn in a year. You can figure out what that would be
in your life, but it's a pretty fair chunk of change on the front
end of the year. The fourth thing to notice is that he gave the servants a clear command: "Put the money to work until I come
back." So, these servants had complete freedom to invest it, cul-
tivate it, and grow it any way they desired. And fifth, there's ac-
countability. The nobleman informs the servants that when he
returns as a king, there will be a day of reckoning. Now, Jesus
doesn't say how long the nobleman was gone; maybe it was a
few months; maybe it was few years. But when he returns as
king, he's not in a playing mood. He sends for his servants and
he orders them to give an account of their investment. According
to the parable, the servants gave three different reports. The first
servant stepped forward and reported, "I multiplied my original
investment ten times!" And the nobleman praises him by saying,
"Well done; good job." The second servant multiplied his original investment five times, and the nobleman responded, "Awesome–keep up the good work." But when we come to the third
servant, things start to get interesting because he didn't do anything with his initial investment. He kept it hidden in his sock
drawer. He didn't lose the mina; he didn't steal the mina; he simply returned what he had been given. But the nobleman wasn't
happy. In fact, he condemns the servant and calls him "wicked."
That's quite a statement. If he had taken the mina and gone to
Vegas, I can see that as wicked. If he had spent his mina on porn
or drugs, I'd consider that wicked. Or if he hired a hitman to take
out his wife, that would fall into the category of wickedness. If
he had invested, made millions, but kept it for himself, I'd consider that wicked. But he didn't do any of those things. He just
returned what he'd been given. Why would that be wicked?

Well, the servant was declared wicked when what he did was measured against what he could have done. If we fail to achieve our God-given potential, we might consider it a tragedy, but never wicked. Yet this parable teaches us that God views this much more seriously than we do. And so, what Jesus is saying in the parable is this: If we choose to sit on what God has entrusted to us and not use it for what it was intended to be used for, the building of His Kingdom, we are wicked.

There are some obvious lessons to learn from this simple parable as it relates to us being stewards of what we've been given. First, we have to remember that when we invest in God's Kingdom, it's an eternal investment of *his* resources, not *ours*. He cares about his resources, so we'd better handle them with care. Second, Jesus is reminding us that we will ultimately give account to God for how we managed his resources. One day, as Christians, we're going to stand before Jesus, the Master. And He's going to ask us one question: "What did you do with what I gave you?" And I'll warn you ahead of time, He won't be impressed by your degrees, salary, the number of cars in your driveway or the size of your home. None of that is going to impress him, and if we take our cues from the world around us, we'll be tragically misled.

By the way, we have been given clear instructions as to how to invest. The Bible teaches that we are to invest in people. God's agenda is people and as we've learned, people are not a means to an end, people are the end. I'm glad that, as churches, we can build buildings, but it is not about buildings. Buildings are a place to inhabit people; they are a means to an end. I'm glad we have great programs, but it's not about programs. Programs are a means to the end. At the end of the day, it's all about people.

Now, I've been doing this a long time. I've been in ministry for thirty-seven years, and here's my fear: I'm afraid that most of us take what God has given us to invest in others and we invest it in ourselves. Maybe we decide to hang onto it because, you never know, we may need it one day. In other words, what if we invest in the Kingdom of God and then something bad happens? What if we lose our job or the stock market crashes? After all, it's better to be safe than sorry. Well, that was the problem with the wicked servant in Jesus' story. It wasn't that he lost what he was given. The problem was that he held onto it, just in case. Like many of us, he was afraid of the unknown. In fact, his fear of the unknown was greater than his fear of the known, and the known was that the king would return some day, and hold the servant accountable.

The point of Jesus' parable is very clear: When Jesus returns to this earth, we are all going to have some one-on-one time with Him, and He is going to ask us, "What did you do with the time I gave you? What did you do with the treasure I gave you? What did you do with the talent that I gave you?" As sure as Jesus came that first time, two thousand years ago, as a baby in Bethlehem, He is coming the second time. And I know He's been away a long time, but if we're going to base our eternity on Jesus' first coming, we had better be prepared for His second coming.

There are many things I don't know and there are many things I can't predict. I don't know what's going to happen to the economy or how long I'll live, but I do know that I'm going to give an account of my life to Jesus. And when I stand before Him, He's going to want to know, "Mike, what did you do with what I gave you? How has my Kingdom benefited because of what I entrusted to you?" So, I would be a fool, as a follower of Jesus, to live my life based on what might happen when Jesus has made it very clear what is going to happen.

So, here's my question to you: "Are you living your life each day with an eternal perspective?" Is there anybody in your life, other than your family, (family doesn't count) that you're investing in for that person's sake?" If you can't think of anyone, then you are not investing your life; you're spending your life. It's interesting, the same Greek word used in the New Testament for "spending" is also translated "wasting."

Investing in this life is like investing in a company that we know is going to go out of business. We may get a dividend here and there, but eventually we're going to lose all of our investment. We only get so much time. Even 100 years—it is still only a matter of time. And the statistics on death are quite definitive. One-out-of-one people die.

The challenge from Jesus is He calls us to see life from an eternal perspective and use our time, treasure, and talent accordingly. He promises if we'll do that, He'll reward us more than we could ever imagine. But many people cannot live life His way because they are afraid of the unknown. Don't reach the end of your life only to discover that your fear kept you from reaching your full Kingdom potential.

There's more to this life than just living and working and trying to make it through the day until you die. If that's all there is, we all should be depressed. If that's all there is, we should drink more, eat more, and be merry more. But here is the good news: Jesus came to give us life and He came to give it abundantly.

Let me warn you that if you live this way, you will seem a bit weird to the world. You will give more than will make sense. You will serve others, rather than only yourself and your own. But to those of us who know that there is an eternity and that one day we are going to stand before God and give an account, making these adjustments is one of the most sensible decisions we can make in this life. And that's what God is looking for— those who are willing to look beyond this life and make adjustments for what we know is to come.

I think C.T. Studd summed it up best when he wrote: "Only one life, twill soon be past, only what's done for Christ will last."

Chapter 5
The Value of Contentment

L ike many churches across America, Hope is made up of several campuses. One of our campuses was built to be a community center throughout the week, not just a sanctuary for Christians on the weekend. We have a coffee shop, indoor and outdoor playgrounds, childhood learning centers, community meeting rooms, basketball and volleyball courts, plus a state-of-the-art fitness center.

About the fitness center: I had finished working out one morning, when a woman who works there walked up and said, "My husband and I were talking, and we don't understand how Hope does what it does."

She elaborated:

We have raised millions of dollars so we could open this new facility, we've built a worship center in Northern Uganda for an orphan village, and we've drilled wells while starting churches all over the Central African Republic so that the lives of those individuals can be changed now and for all eternity. After the recent hurricane hit Haiti, we took an offering and collected $130,000 to send to our campus in Port-au-Prince for hurricane relief. Last week, $100,000 in cash was given to us as part of the Mina Project to invest and grow so we could give it away to fulfill a need in the community. How in the world is it possible for us to do all that we do?

Well, the answer may or may not surprise you. It has nothing to do with the fact that our church family gets to live in one of the wealthiest areas in the world. It has nothing to do with the growth of the stock market (although, that doesn't hurt). The level to which we are able to impact the community we live in and the world around us is directly related to the level of contentment in our lives.

When I think about contentment, I don't know that anybody ever modeled this trait better than the Apostle Paul. He never allowed circumstances to control his attitude. He didn't let the threat of death or prison or the possibility of prosperity affect him. Regardless of what Paul went through, he figured out how to be content. This is what he said when he wrote a letter to the church at Philippi.

"I am not saying this because I am in need, for I have learned to be content whatever the circumstances. I know what it is to be in need, and I know what it is to have plenty. I have learned the secret of being content in any and every situation, whether well fed or hungry, whether living in plenty or in want. I can do all this through Him who gives me strength." (Philippians 4:11-13)

By the way, when Paul wrote this letter, he wasn't being a drama queen. Paul's life was a roller coaster. There were times of prosperity and there were times of poverty, but it didn't seem to matter which one he was experiencing. He didn't assume God had forgotten him when he was sleeping on the street with a growling stomach, nor did he overlook the role God played in his life when he had a roof over his head and three meals a day to enjoy. Regardless of his circumstances, he always found a way to be content.

So, here's another question for you (and don't act shocked; you knew it was coming). Have you discovered how to be content, regardless of your circumstances?

Let's talk contentment. Contentment means that we're happy with what we have and we're happy with our life. Here's a good test that works for me: If you were to remain exactly where you are for the rest of your life, would you be okay with that? For example, if your finances never improve and you never advance in your career, would you be content? If you never own your dream home or your dream car, would you be content? If God never allows you to marry and start a family, would you be content?

Part of the problem is that we live in a culture where we are reminded every day of what we don't have and what we're missing. For example, we're constantly reminded of how outdated our technology has become. We buy the new iPhone 137, and two weeks later the new iPhone 138 comes out. We feel our phone is outdated. We feel our wardrobe and our car is outdated, and we're discontented. The problem with discontentment is that it's an appetite that is never fully satisfied.

So, what do you do with that appetite? Satisfying an appetite doesn't make it go away. We've all eaten a hardy breakfast, only to find ourselves starving by mid-morning. We finally make it to noon and head to the closest Golden Corral, belly up to the trough; an hour later, we waddle to our car wondering if gluttony really is a sin, but by mid-afternoon, we're hungry again! In the same way, we will never amass enough in this life to be content and not want more. Likewise, it seems the more we have, the more we want.

Let me illustrate this with a personal story. A few years ago, I wanted to buy a new truck. I looked at some of the newer models but wasn't thrilled with the price tag or the options. The salesman offered to keep an eye out for a used truck with a better price and all the bells and whistles. One day he called and told me that someone had traded in a truck that he thought I'd be interested in. I took one look at it and bought it without even a test drive. It was a platinum edition with low miles and it was loaded! It had interior lighting that changed colors, leather seats, nice wheels and tires, running boards that slide out when the doors open, and a pearl white exterior. It was perfect. That is until I rode in my friend's truck. He had a new truck, fully-loaded—the leather was soft and the truck smelled new. It was nicer than my truck; I wanted a new truck. I was ready to trade in my truck for another. Was it because there was something wrong with my truck? No.

The more we have, the more we want.

And when we live that way, it short-circuits our ability to be content. So how do we curb our appetite for more? How do we get a handle on our lack of contentment?

In 1 Timothy 6, we get some answers to this challenge in a letter that was written by the Apostle Paul to a young man, Timothy, with whom Paul was in a mentoring relationship, preparing him for the ministry. Paul makes this statement in 1 Timothy 6:6-7: "But godliness with contentment is great gain. For we brought nothing into the world, and we can take nothing out of it."

We all know that. None of us has seen a hearse pulling a U-Haul, yet it doesn't stop us from living as if our lives depend on what we have, own, possess.

Paul continues in 1 Timothy 6:8: "But if we have food and clothing, we will be content with that." Keep in mind, this was written in the first century during a time when the poverty was so severe that people lived each day wondering if they were going to eat a meal, much less three. An average person's wardrobe consisted of what they were wearing, and they typically wore that outfit until it "wore" out, and only then would they get another. There's wisdom to what Paul wrote to Timothy. We probably should be content if we have enough to eat today and if we have clothes to wear today, anything more is icing on the cake. (By the way, I didn't get a new truck.)

Yet there's something inside of us, especially Americans, that is never satisfied. No matter how much we have, we want more. We want to be rich! By the way, odds are that 99% of those who are reading this are already rich. At the time of writing, the average household income in the United States is about $51,200. The average household income worldwide is $9,733. That means a household income of $32,400 a year places one in the 1% of the richest people on the planet. Many, if not most of us, fall into that category. If that's the case, you may want to put down this book and call your family and friends to let them know that you're rich, in case they need anything. Let me know how that works out for you!

In 1 Timothy 6:9 Paul warns, "Those who want to get rich fall into temptation and a trap and into many foolish and harmful desires that plunge people into ruin and destruction." And that sounds ominous, but we all know it's true. We all know people who have ruined their lives due to material pursuits. Maybe their credit was so good, they were able to borrow more than was wise, or they lived on 110% of their income and amassed debilitating debt. Or maybe it's simply because, no matter how much they had, it was never enough. We need to understand that when we have more than we need, there are temptations we would never fall prey to if we didn't have more than we needed. If our goal in life is to be rich, watch out because boundaries will be needed to keep us away from the pitfalls only experienced by the very wealthy.

Some people have strayed from their faith because of the pursuit of riches. 1 Timothy 6:10 says, "For the love of money is a root of all kinds of evil. Some people, eager for money, have wandered from the faith and pierced themselves with many griefs."

You may have wandered away from your relationship with God to pursue wealth, but you are back and maybe you are back because God took it all away to bring you back. Maybe you finally hit a wall and you realized the pursuit of wealth was going nowhere fast. I once had a man say to me, "I've made millions of dollars and lost every penny of it seven times over." He understands the greed of which Paul is speaking.

Paul also gives us the practical side of this pursuit in 1 Timothy 6:11-12, "But you, man of God, flee from all this, and pursue righteousness, godliness, faith, love, endurance and gentleness. Fight the good fight of the faith. Take hold of the eternal life to which you were called when you made your good confession in the presence of many witnesses."

It may not be obvious to you, but Paul, in those two verses, tells us how to deal with our lack of contentment. He says that if we have more than we need, and that's most of us, we have to make a conscious decision to turn from the pursuit of wealth and pursue something else. We have to make an intentional decision to re-channel our desire for more and take all of that emotion and energy that we were putting toward the material pursuit and begin to pursue, to redirect ourselves toward something altogether different.

Paul gives us some specifics on how to do this beginning in 1 Timothy 6:17: "Command those who are rich in this present world not to be arrogant nor to put their hope in wealth, which is so uncertain, but to put their hope in God, who richly provides us with everything for our enjoyment." And that's good news because if you are rich by this world's standard, Paul says, "God gave it to you to enjoy!" If God has blessed you with a beach house, enjoy it! If you get to be a member of a country club, enjoy it! If you have a mountain vacation home, enjoy it! If you get to drive nice cars and live in a nice house, enjoy them! Enjoy being rich in this present world, but do not make the pursuit of such your chief pursuit.

And then Paul becomes more specific in 1 Timothy 6:18: "Command them to do good, to be rich in good deeds..."

What that means is that we are to use our extra time and

money intentionally and purposefully to help other people. In other words, when someone looks at your life, instead of being amazed by what you have, they should be amazed by what you've *done* with what you have.

1 Timothy 6:19 says, "In this way they will lay up treasure for themselves as a firm foundation for the coming age, so that they may take hold of the life that is truly life." Paul warns those of us that are living the dream to be careful that we don't miss out on true life. In other words, we're not to focus on pursuing more and bigger and better and shinier and newer because that pursuit will always be unfulfilling.

Instead, Paul tells Timothy to tell the rich people to do good and be rich in good deeds. Be generous with what God has given you and be willing to share. If we will leverage our good fortune in this manner, we will experience what it means to truly live. As a bonus, we will avoid the pitfalls that accompany being wealthy. For that to happen, we must flee the pursuit of more and more wealth and intentionally pursue another way of handling our wealth.

Of course, we can't get up one day and decide to be content. We've all tried to do that to no avail. We can't pretend we don't want what we really want. We can't avoid the mall forever; we can't ignore the sales and the commercials, but we can learn to manage our appetite. The New Testament teaches that strategic generosity curbs our greed and puts a bridle on our discontentment.

Personally, I teach the biblical principle of priority percentage giving. I'm going to give away a percentage of my income, and I believe the Bible teaches 10%; before I spend it on myself, based on the principle of first fruits. When I get paid, I bring the first 10% back to God and learn to live within my means.

When Laura and I were first married and bought our first home, we borrowed mattresses from her parents and slept on the floor for a year because we couldn't afford to buy a bed. Even though we were living that way, we knew we were supposed to be tithing, yet we weren't. A friend shared the principle to tithe first, then learn how to live on the rest. That is a principle that we started thirty-nine years ago and it still works to this day. To paraphrase the New Testament, that kind of giving curbs our appetite for more, and it bridles our discontentment. That's the value of strategic generosity.

Though we live in a culture where we are constantly reminded of what we don't have, we seem to have to go out of our way to discover what other people don't have. If we are blindly pursuing our own riches, we will never be aware of anybody else's need. For most of us, nobody's knocking on our front door asking for money or food, nor is anyone sleeping on the sidewalk in front of our house. My guess is that most of us don't even have a peripheral relationship with a genuinely poor person. That's the culture in which we live. And to be honest, most of us would prefer to keep it that way because if we don't see it, we can pretend it doesn't exist.

So how do we counteract this situation? The only way I know is to intentionally make decisions that will bring us into an awareness of other's needs. That is why I will forever be grateful for the opportunity God has given me to visit third-world countries. I've traveled to the Central African Republic where the average household income was $240 a year. Can you imagine trying to live on $20 a month?

Here are some eye-opening facts:

The people in Bangui, CAR, still live in mud huts and go to the creek to get their water. They spend 99% of their time, each day, trying to secure a single meal.

The majority of the population of Uganda is under the age of 15 because of a civil war and the AIDS epidemic. Many of them are orphans. Outside of the main cities, people live in shacks without running water or electricity.

In Port-au-Prince, Haiti, three and a half million people live in a space originally planned for 100,000, and they live in poverty.

I'm so thankful to God for allowing me to see this because when I experienced it, my mind was immediately taken from what I don't have (and don't need) to what *they* don't have but do *need*. It happened automatically.

We need to become aware of those around us. Most of us live in a bubble, so for that to happen, we have to do some homework.

Laura has supported many orphans in Uganda, Central African Republic, and Haiti. We send away $35 a month and it guarantees a child food, school, clothing, and medical care. We receive letters from the orphans reporting on how they're doing. I've even had the opportunity to meet with some of the children we're sponsoring when visiting their country. Maybe you have done that already. You have put their picture on your refrigerator and, as a family, you pray for them. If you have not sponsored a child, I encourage you to do this. It will remind you that there are people with needs that aren't being met. Take your family on a mission trip so your kids can see there's more to life than what they see in their surroundings. Take bottles of water and food to an inner city, and minister to the needs of your own community. Get to know the poverty in your area.

A couple years ago Laura and I were on our way to Uganda. We got as far as London; We were checking in when they said, "Mr. Lee, you can't go because you only have four months left on your passport, and you must have six months left on your passport to enter the country." I called the embassy. I did everything I could to make it work. They said, "No." Plan B.

I knew I wasn't preaching that weekend so I could be like a real person and do something fun. We decided to fly to JFK and spend a couple of days in New York City. It was Valentine's Day so we planned to go to a Broadway show and enjoy a romantic dinner. We landed; it was so cold! We got a hotel and tried for a Broadway show; however, to get tickets, especially last minute, costs a fortune. We passed on it and went straight for the romantic dinner. The next morning, we woke up to a temperature of two degrees Fahrenheit. We bundled up and headed out to breakfast. Everywhere we walked, we saw homeless people sleeping in doorways or leaning against buildings. One man had an umbrella over him and a newspaper under him in an attempt to avoid the elements. I tried to speak to him, but he didn't respond; I thought he was dead. Finally, he opened his eyes. We gave him some money for a hot meal. Laura and I were so amazed at the number of people sleeping on the streets that we went to an ATM and withdrew a good amount of cash. Instead of going to a Broadway show, we went around giving money to the homeless. It didn't fix their problems, but it is what God laid on our hearts to do. The point is, if we were not made aware of these cold and needy people, we would have never been moved to respond, and this applies to all of us. We must become aware of the needs of others.

What are you going to do to make sure that your children don't grow up thinking it's all about what they don't have? Again, I'm telling you that generosity bridles our discontentment and curbs our appetite for more.

There are incredible benefits to embracing this biblical lifestyle. You'll be better off financially because you'll be living within your means; somebody else will be better off financially because they have been helped, and the Kingdom of God will be better off financially. Everybody wins.

If that's not motivation enough, remember the words of John 3:16: "For God so loved the world that He gave His one and only Son, that whoever believes in Him shall not perish but have eternal life." Follow God's example of generosity so that God can use us to change the world. Fight discontentment with generosity. Focus on the eternal.

Chapter 6
Balancing Grace and Truth

What's the one thing that the Christian has to offer to the world that the world can't get anywhere else? Think about it: You don't have to be a Christian to feed the hungry or help the poor, even though we should. You don't have to be a Christian to build medical clinics in poverty-stricken countries around the world. Other groups and organizations are very effective at that kind of thing. There are other traditions and teachers that offer wise, moral instructions about how to be a better citizen of planet earth. So, what's the one thing that you, as a Christian, have to offer the world that the world can't get anywhere else?

Philip Yancey writes in his book, *What's So Amazing About Grace*, "The one thing that the world cannot do is it cannot offer grace. It cannot say to human beings, 'You are lost, but now you're found. You were guilty, but now you've been pardoned. You were dead, but now you've been made alive.'"

And the Bible has a lot to say about grace. For example, the Apostle Paul talked about grace when he wrote to that small group of Christians in Colossae. Colossians 2:13-14: "When you were dead in your sins and in the uncircumcision of your flesh, God made you alive with Christ. He forgave us all our sins, having canceled the charge of our legal indebtedness, which stood against us and condemned us; he has taken it away, nailing it to the cross."

The phrase that caught my attention is: "Having canceled the charge of our legal indebtedness, which stood against us and condemned us …" We have this huge moral debt and we don't have the funds, resources, or means to cover it. But Paul reminds us that God took our indebtedness, guilt, and shame and nailed it to the cross. And when He did, God not only erased our debt, he destroyed the certificate. In other words, he ripped up the "IOU" so that we're free and clean and unburdened, and it's all because grace that has been extended to us.

Which brings me to a question: If this amazing grace that's been extended to us is the one unique thing that Christians have to offer the world, then why don't we do a better job of offering it? How is it that our churches are filled with people who sing about grace and say they've been saved by grace, and yet be so ungracious? You may say, "Well, I don't think that's true; I think you're over-reacting." If you feel that way, let me give you a challenge. Next time you leave the safety of your home and head out into the world, find someone who doesn't go to church (that shouldn't be too hard). It could be a neighbor, a co-worker, or maybe a family member. Ask them what they associate with the word, "Christian" and see what they say. They'll use words like judgmental, self-righteousness, prideful, but I promise you that you will not hear the word, grace. Do you know why? Because even we've been extended grace, we have a hard time extending grace to other people. In other words, we have a hard time being gracious.

Do you know what I think the problem is? I think that it's pride. I think that when we're desperate and we know that we're lost without hope, we're open to the idea of grace. We know that we need grace and so we want grace. But once we become Christians and we're not desperate anymore, we start to feel pretty good about ourselves. We start to feel that God got a pretty good deal when he got us. Over time we slowly forget what our lives were like without God. We think, "Maybe I wasn't that bad to start with." And before long, there's a pride thing (it's called self-righteousness in the Bible) that convinces us that we're better than other people. And as a result, we begin to see ourselves as qualified to sit judging "those poor sinners" who aren't as enlightened as we are.

Before you know it, even though we are saved by grace, grace slowly gets choked out of our lives. Then it becomes "us vs. them;" or "the good guys vs. the bad guys." But if our hearts actually reflected the heart of God, they would be filled with compassion, love, and grace towards everyone we see. There would be no more "us vs. them." We would see every person as someone that Christ died for and deserves His grace. We would realize that people we interact with everyday matter to God. We would grasp that He loves them as much as He loves us and that His Son also died for them. We would be reminded that God's desire is to reach them and redeem them. We would comprehend that God has a heart of grace that's huge and indiscriminately loving.

Now, I'm going to let you in on a secret that anybody that's been around Christians for a while already knows; in fact, it's kind of an unspoken understanding among Christians. Here it is: It's OK to raise hell and be a really extravagant sinner as long as you're an outsider who's never been an insider. And the reason that it's OK is that if you ever decide to follow Christ, you'll make a great story. We will definitely interview you at a church service. Heck, we may even make a video about your miraculous transformation. But once you've been on the inside, you can kiss that kind of forgiveness and acceptance good-bye, because now when you sin, you're making us all look bad and we have no other option than to take you down. And no matter how much you repent and how sorry you are, it's on your permanent record.

Now that would be the common church position. The problem is, I don't think Jesus held the same opinion. After all, He's the one who said that it's not healthy people who need a doctor or a hospital; it's people who are sick. So, one of my biggest frustrations with Christians is that when fellow Christians stumble, instead of helping, we often shoot our wounded. For example, somebody in the church family gets off course and their marriage blows up or maybe an old habit resurfaces. Maybe they have kids that are rebellious and wayward.

Those of us who have kids know that until kids can get around, things go pretty smoothly, but once they start crawling, it all goes downhill from there. Sure, between the ages of one and six there are a couple of good days. And there are even a few fleeting moments when you think you might be raising a little angel. Then one day the school calls, and you ask yourself, "Where did my angel go?" Next, they become teenagers and appear to be possessed by Satan, himself. Up until this point, you thought you were doing OK as a mom, dad. But now you have this adolescent who wants to spread his or her wings and before you know it, they're making poor decisions and they're getting in trouble. Some people smile and assure you that they're praying for you, but you know what everyone is really saying behind closed doors. Trust me on this; I've been there.

Maybe it wasn't your marriage or your child that blew up; maybe it was you. And other Christians turned their back on you. This is where Christians often times blow it. There's something inside of us that feels that justice means that the person has to get what he deserves. But when we live like that, we need to understand it does not show the heart of God.

Take that person that you absolutely cannot stand (get a mental picture in your mind). Now be honest, the last place you want to see that person is at the same church you attend. But what would it look like if we, instead of gossiping, judging or taking pot shots, responded, "I've got to help – I've got to get involved. I've got to get this person to a place where they can receive nurture and care."

What if the first thought was, "I've got to get this person to Jesus! He's the Great Physician. He's the one that can heal and redeem and restore." And what if you brought that person into the fold where they could learn to live life victoriously and stay out of the deep weeds? That's an attitude that would show the heart of God. Like God, you would have a heart of grace that's huge and indiscriminately loving.

One of the greatest examples of this kind of grace is recorded in John 8. It all began early one morning in the city of Jerusalem. A small group of people had gathered in a Bible study Jesus was teaching. (How cool would that be?) And all of a sudden, a handful of angry and hate-filled men interrupted Jesus. They are the self-righteous men of the city; they are the scribes and the Pharisees. But these men also had someone with them who didn't fit in. It was a woman who is never named here or any-where else in the Bible. Her hair was probably disheveled; her make-up smeared. Maybe her clothes were torn. Her arm may have been bruised or cut from the struggle. I'm sure that every-one in this small Bible study was stunned by the interruption, but according to John 8, Jesus calmly listens to the accusations.

In John 8:4-5 it says, "Teacher, this woman was caught in the act of adultery. In the Law Moses commanded us to stone such women. Now what do you say?"

There was no question she was guilty. She was caught in the very act and the Law called for her execution. But Jesus, observ-ing the scene, doesn't miss a clue. In fact, He knows exactly what's going on. According to John 8:6, Jesus knew that they were using this as a trap. The people attending the Bible study didn't know it. The woman didn't know it. But Jesus knew ex-actly what was going on; He was well acquainted with these re-ligious snobs and He knew how they operated.

He knew that if He said, "Stone her," they would call Him a hypocrite because He was building His following by preaching a message of compassion, forgiveness, love, and grace. If that was His platform, how can He now say, "Kill her; stone her?" That would send a mixed message.

The only other option was to say, "Let her go." But then they could accuse Him of breaking the Law of Moses; they could even say that He condoned adultery, that He's easy on sinners. And when you get to verse 6, Jesus does something that I'm sure made no sense whatsoever. Jesus stooped and began writing in the dirt. I used to think that He was buying time by doodling in the dirt so he could come up with an answer. But because of the way the confrontation shifts, I believe that Jesus began to write, large enough for them to read, a list of their secret, hidden sins: Greed, lust, pride, jealousy, envy…adultery. You see, I think it was a set-up from the beginning. This isn't something you just stumble across early one morning while you're taking a walk. Every precaution takes place to make sure that the illicit act remains private. Drapes are drawn. Doors are locked. They bring the woman to Jesus, but where is the man? It takes two to tango. Is a man that's caught in the act of adultery any less guilty than a woman that's caught in the act of adultery? Not according to the Law. That's why I think it was a setup. In fact, I wonder if the man who had committed adultery with her was now standing as one of her accusers.

The silence broke in John 8:7 when Jesus stands up, looks into their faces and says, "If you've got it all together, take the first shot; throw the first stone." "Just make sure that your hearts are pure, spotless—and then throw it."

Can you imagine the tension? You could hear a pin drop. He looked at them; they were silent. They thought about their lives, hearts. They let the confrontation pass in review. And in John 8:9, they drop their stones, one by one, and slip away - just like you would—just like I would. Why? Because they were not qualified to judge this woman—and none of us would be qualified either.

The scene that follows is a study in contrast. Jesus was left alone with this woman.

He looks directly into the eyes of one who deserved death

but saved from it by the only One who was qualified to judge her. I would love to have seen her face. There she stood and there He stood, and their eyes locked. I doubt you could invent a more contrasting scene—as out of place as Lady Gaga at a convent. A woman, a man. A sinner, the sinless Son of God. An adulteress, the Messiah.

In John 8:10, Jesus straightened up and asked her, "Woman, where are they? Has no one condemned you?" And the only recorded words of this woman found in the Bible are in John 8:11 when she says, "No one, sir."

Isn't that a great moment? I think she even included herself in that statement. I think that for the first time in her life she understood what freedom from the shame and awful guilt of her life felt like. "No one, sir—not even me—I don't even condemn myself."

And His marvelous response in John 8:11 was the perfect balance of grace and truth: "Then neither do I condemn you," Jesus declared. "Go now and leave your life of sin." That's what Jesus says to the woman, and that's what the woman believes. She is able to go and change her entire lifestyle because she is the recipient of truth balanced with grace. But that doesn't mean she didn't continue to need grace.

You see, often we fall into the trap of thinking that grace is what saves us, and then that's the end of grace. In fact, I used to wish that God would change me permanently. Now don't get me wrong, there are some areas in my life I've always been pretty strong in. For example, I've never had the desire to rob liquor stores or banks. Arson has never tempted me—neither has hijacking. In fact, my behavior has always been pretty impeccable in those areas. But honestly, it goes downhill from there.

And because I have so many issues, I wanted my transformation to be so deep and so permanent that even if God died, I'd still be Godly. I wanted my spiritual transformation to be

more like Spider-Man. Spider-Man was instantaneously transformed by a spider bite. The theme song goes: "Spider-man, Spider-Man, does whatever a spider can." And that's what I wanted
God to do to me. I wanted Him to land on me and bite my soul
in such a way that it would make me fall down and get back up
as "Godly-Man." I wanted to get up each day and sing: "Godly-
Man, Godly-Man, does whatever a Godly man can."

But spiritual transformation isn't like that; it's much messier.

That's why the woman in John 8 received more than just
grace – she was also the recipient of truth. Jesus gave her grace
when He said, "I don't condemn you, even though I could." He
shared truth when He said, "Now, clean up your act and change
your ways."

Spiritual transformation is a daily practice of experiencing
grace and applying truth. And that means that grace can't be a
yesterday, or last week, or when-I-first-came-to-Christ experience. It's like the manna that God provided the Israelites in the
wilderness. It had to be fresh to be edible. In the same way, we
need fresh grace balanced with timeless truth to experience the
transformation it brings.

That's why we need a grace that, not only saves us, we also
need a grace that keeps us. It's the truth of God's word that
changes us. It's learning to live within the laws, principles, pre-
cepts, and parameters of God's Word. It's the grace of God that
keeps us going, day by day.

But this is what breaks my heart: there are thousands of broken people living all around us without a relationship with God.
And the reason they're out there and not in the Kingdom of God
is because of the imbalance of grace and truth. I believe that
there are all kinds of people in our community who would love
to have a relationship with Jesus and long to experience his love,
grace, forgiveness, and peace. And, just so you know, the problem isn't Jesus. No one ever has anything bad to say about Jesus.
The problem is us; they can't stand Christians and what, at least

from their perspective, we represent. They see us as judgmental, hypocritical, prideful, and self-righteous.

So how do we become people of grace and truth?

1st: We have to remember where we've come from. Do you know why I can show grace to others? Because when I am intensely aware of my own shortcomings, it's a lot harder to be judgmental about other people. I need to be reminded that it's my IOU that's nailed to that cross.

Can you imagine if in Jesus' day you actually lived within viewing distance of where the crucifixion took place? Every day as you walked out your front door you would be reminded that he died for your sins. How gracious, tolerant would you be towards others?

I urge you to write out the word "grace" and put it someplace as a reminder of how grace saved you and keeps you and how truth is changing you. And will help remind you that other people need grace and truth, too.

2nd: We need to be grace-providing people. Let's face it, we all need some people in our lives that accept us and love us no matter what. We need these grace-providing people because we'll always have some grace-impaired people in our lives. And by grace-impaired, I mean people who judge us and look down their noses at the things they don't approve of.

I have tattoos. (I can just feel the smug, judgmental attitudes that are thinking: "I would never…") Forget tattoos; that's a silly example. But if you discover that a person you know is struggling in an area of his or her life, do you really think it helps to remind them that you would never do that? How you answer that question will determine if you're a grace-provider, or if you're grace-impaired.

Where do you draw the line when it comes to grace? If someone is gay, does that cross the line? What if someone has an abortion or has filed for bankruptcy or is a convicted felon or a sex-offender? What if they struggle with some form of addiction? Where do you refuse to drop the stone? At that point, you're grace-impaired.

My Christian journey hasn't exactly been characterized by grace. I grew up in an incredibly legalistic church. Our mission statement was, "Us four and no more!" We separated ourselves from sinners to the fourth degree. I couldn't hang out with anyone that knew anyone that knew anyone that sinned. And then, to reinforce my upbringing, I attended one of the most legalistic, judgmental Christian universities in the United States. They even had issues with Billy Graham.

But being a grace-provider doesn't mean that you avoid the truth. It means that when good things happen, you celebrate. It also means that when you see the darkness and sin in someone, you are not repelled or repulsed. In fact, the opposite is true. Love forces you to move towards that person and speak truth into that person's life.

3rd: We need to find people who need grace and truth and extend it to them. This is what Jesus loved to do more than anything else. He loved to extend grace to people - especially people who knew they didn't deserve it. He loved to speak truth into the lives of those who were lost and confused. That practice got Him into trouble but it brought such great joy to those who were the recipient.

I mentioned earlier that I understood how parents feel when they are judged by their children's actions. I know how judgmental looks and gossip can discourage you and beat you up as a parent. Pastor's kids live under a microscope and the people that attend church with them often scrutinize them. Everyone knows who they are and everyone thinks that they are qualified to speak truth to them.

But only the few that love you and your children have the

right to share the sorrows and pain that you go through as a parent with a wayward child. Friends and family that understand their failings as a parent can offer love and support during times of worry. The people who pray for your child and you as a parent show God's indiscriminate grace and love during times that can break a family apart.

Laura and I will be forever grateful to a couple that attended our church while our boys were teenagers. Jim and Pat listened, loved, prayed and showed grace. They sat with us while we cried and tried to figure out what we had done wrong. They didn't justify our son's actions or applaud our parenting. They never passed judgment; they extended grace. They showed us the graciousness of Jesus. It helped us keep our sanity and to never lose hope. It made all the difference in the world in our lives.

Today, God is looking for people who will extend grace to people who don't deserve it. He is looking for people to love and show grace to the wounded. He is waiting for us to bring others to the Great Physician.

Chapter 7

The Ball is in Your Court

You may have gotten to this point in the book and you heartily agree with everything you've read. You understand that God wants to use you. You understand that He doesn't expect you to have all of the answers. You understand that your usability isn't based on your talent or skill or education or pedigree. You understand that God doesn't expect you to have it all together financially. Your family doesn't have to be perfect (even though we do our best to make it look that way on social media). In fact, some of the best examples of family dysfunction you will ever read about are found in the Bible. The Bible is full of people who had plenty of issues (Jesus' family tree was scandalous), but God still used them to do unbelievable things—and we know that. So, what does that mean to you right now? What is God moving you to do right now? How does He want to use you right now, warts and all? Whatever it is, my guess is, based on years of experience, it is not your lack of skill or talent that's keeping you from going forward with God. My guess is that it's fear. And the fear is probably based on the fact that what God is moving you to do doesn't make any sense whatsoever, and I get it.

I've followed Jesus long enough to know that there are times in our lives when God will ask us to do something on our journey of faith that doesn't make any sense. In fact, sometimes God asks us to do something that seems to be the exact opposite of what we think we need to do. For example, in the Bible, God asks us to give. He doesn't say, "If you can afford it, give." He doesn't say, "When you get out of debt, give." He doesn't say,

"When your retirement is secure and you have lots of expend-able income, give." He just says, "Give." Often our response is, "I don't even have enough money to make ends meet as it is; how do you expect me to give? It doesn't make any sense what-soever."

Or maybe you're in a marriage and it's a disaster. All your bitter girlfriends whose marriages are also disasters keep telling you to cut your losses and get out. But you read the Bible and it says that God hates divorce and that He wants you to fight for your marriage. But you look at your circumstances and think, "That doesn't make any sense whatsoever." My point is, as Christians, there are those critical times in our lives when God will ask us to do certain things that don't make any sense. But I want to share a principle with you that has the potential to change your life: God is a very reasonable God. And God doesn't ask us to do anything that doesn't make sense *from his perspective.* In fact, what we're learning in this book is that God always has a reason. And more often than not, if we'll obey God and do what He's asking us, we'll have one of those "Aha–now I get it" moments. Sometimes we won't understand why God asks us to do what He wants us to do until after we decide whether or not we're going to obey God.

A perfect example of this principle is in the life of Abraham. God tells Abram (later to become Abraham) in Genesis 12:1-3, "Go from your country, your people and your father's house-hold to the land I will show you. I will make you into a great na-tion, and I will bless you; I will make your name great, and you will be a blessing. I will bless those who bless you, and whoever curses you I will curse; and all peoples on earth will be blessed through you." That was the promise that God made to Abraham. It was the promise that not only would God bring a new nation through Abraham, God would also bring the Messiah through his lineage so that "all peoples on earth will be blessed through you." And Abraham responded in faith by going on the journey and traveling to the Promised Land.

Later on, we read in Genesis 15:1-3: After this, the word of the Lord came to Abram in a vision: "Do not be afraid, Abram. I am your shield, your very great reward."

But Abram said, "Sovereign Lord, what can you give me since I remain childless and the one who will inherit my estate is Eliezer of Damascus?"

And Abram said, "You have given me no children; so, a servant in my household will be my heir."

As I just mentioned, God has already promised Abraham that he would be a father to the people of God and a blessing to all the nations. But Abraham realizes that the odds of that happening are pretty low if you don't have any children, and so Abraham points that out to God. "Then the word of the Lord came to him: 'This man will not be your heir, but a son who is your own flesh and blood will be your heir.' He took him outside and said, 'Look up at the sky and count the stars—if indeed you can count them.' Then He said to him, 'So shall your offspring be.' Abram believed the Lord, and He credited it to him as righteousness." (Genesis 15:4-6)

Now, Abraham was a human being and not a perfect one. He was very fallible. But God says, "I'll now treat you as a righteous person, I'll consider you to be perfect, if you're willing to trust me." In other words, God is willing to accept Abraham's trust in place of Abraham being righteous! Abraham believed and trusted God for the promise and that made his relationship with God possible.

Then, an amazing thing happens. Abraham, the paragon of faith, doesn't exactly trust God. In Genesis 16:1-2 it says, "Now Sarai, Abram's wife, had borne him no children. But she had an Egyptian slave named Hagar; so, she said to Abram, 'The Lord has kept me from having children. Go, sleep with my slave; perhaps I can build a family through her.' Abram agreed to what Sarai said." That's our role model of faith! His decision is a result of his lack of trust in God. Abraham and Sarai weren't able to leave it in God's hands, and so they ran ahead of God and took matters into their own hands, and the result was a great deal of conflict, heartache, pain.

In Genesis 17:1 we read, "When Abram was ninety-nine years old..." By the way, Abraham was seventy-five when God first made his promise to Abraham in Genesis 12. Ishmael was born eleven years later when Abraham was eighty-six. In Genesis 17, it's twenty-four years after God's original promise back in Genesis 12. Imagine what it would be like to wait twenty-four years for a promise, with no result.

Let's continue in Genesis 17:1-6.

"When Abram was ninety-nine years old, the Lord appeared to him and said, 'I am God Almighty; walk before me faithfully and be blameless. Then I will make my covenant between me and you and will greatly increase your numbers.' Abram fell facedown [this is a response of worship] and God said to him, 'As for me, this is my covenant with you: You will be the father of many nations. No longer will you be called Abram; your name will be Abraham, for I have made you a father of many nations. I will make you very fruitful; I will make nations of you, and kings will come from you.'"

This is how Abraham responds in Genesis 17:17. "Abraham fell facedown; he laughed and said to himself, 'Will a son be born to a man a hundred years old? Will Sarah bear a child at the age of ninety?'"

And later on, when Sarah hears the good news, she laughs, too! They're like, "I know you're God and all, but have you checked our birth certificates lately? We're pretty old; we are not spring chickens."

In Genesis 17:19 it says, "Then God said, 'Yes, but your wife

Sarah will bear you a son, and you will call him Isaac. I will establish my covenant with him as an everlasting covenant for his
descendants after him.'"

And, sure enough, we read in Genesis 21:1-3: "Now
the Lord was gracious to Sarah as He had said, and the Lord did
for Sarah what He had promised. Sarah became pregnant and
bore a son to Abraham in his old age, at the very time God had
promised him. Abraham gave the name Isaac to the son Sarah
bore him."

By the way, the Hebrew word for "Isaac" means, "He
laughs!" I mean, God's sheer goodness and graciousness in this
story is an amazing thing. He tells Abraham and Sarah that
they're going to have a son, and Abraham laughs and Sarah
laughs. So, God says, "We'll go with what's working; let's name
the kid, "He laughs.'" This was all possible because Abraham
was willing to leave a life of safety and normalcy, and he was
willing to join with God on the adventure of faith.

There are two things that always strike me as I go through
the story of Abraham. One is the graciousness of God who
makes and keeps these wonderful promises. The second thing
is how human and fallible Abraham is. He screwed up over and
over again and his faith constantly wavered. This brings up the
question: "What kind of faith is God looking for?"

We get some insight into the answer to that question in Genesis 17. God has laid out the covenant for Abraham, and God
says, "I'm committing myself to you without reservation. We're
bound together by an unbreakable promise." Then He goes on
to say to Abraham, "And we'll have a sign, and it will be a reminder of our relationship covenant."

And Abraham was like, "A sign? Great! What will it be?"

And God responds, "Circumcision."

I'm sure Abraham thought, "Couldn't it be something like a
secret password or a special handshake . . . something like that?"
Regardless of what Abraham thought, there's a little four-word

phrase that the writer uses twice in a couple of verses to describe Abraham's response.

Genesis 17:23-26 says, "*On that very day* Abraham took his son Ishmael and all those born in his household or bought with his money, every male in his household, and circumcised them, as God told him. Abraham was ninety-nine years old when he was circumcised, and his son Ishmael was thirteen; Abraham and his son Ishmael were both circumcised *on that very day* [emphasis mine]."

Twice the writer goes out of his way to say, "Not only did Abraham do it, but he did it *on that very day*." Why does he include that phrase? I think it's because he wants us to understand that Abraham immediately, without hesitation, responded to God's commandment. We see this over and over again in the story of Abraham. God says, "Go to this new land," and Abraham leaves everything and goes to the new land. God says, "Circumcision," and Abraham follows through with it *on that very day*. Abraham wasn't perfect. He made mistakes and he struggled with doubt, but he had enough faith to respond to God's command and that was enough for God. Abraham trusted God, and the way we can tell is because he was obedient to God.

So, the question is: What's keeping you from trusting God and being fully obedient to Him? I've discovered that what often prevents me from walking by faith is fear. It's all of the "What if's?" In other words, "What if I do my part, but God doesn't do his part?" It's like when we're trying to teach our kids to swim. I have two boys and I can remember what it was like to stand in the pool and try to get them to jump to me while reassuring them that I was trustworthy and I wouldn't let them drown. There was a phrase I used over and over again, and it's the same phrase that all parents use when we're trying to get our kids to take that step of faith and jump in the pool. We say, "Don't be afraid — just jump." And when we say that, we don't only say it to provide comfort; we also say it to motivate them to take action.

In the same way, in your life, you're going to receive promises and commandments and promptings and nudgings from God. And in order to respond and do what God wants, you're going to have to face fear over and over again.

I want to wrap it all up by encouraging you: Don't let your fear keep you from responding in obedience.

Think about it this way: What kind of trust did I want my boys to have when I was trying to get them to jump in the pool? It didn't have to be 100% certainty of how it was going to turn out. I needed them to trust me enough to jump and I would take care of everything else from my end. And it's because I knew from my perspective as a parent that once they jumped, they would discover that Daddy wasn't going to let them drown after all.

It works the same way when it comes to our relationship with God. Once we take action and obey what God is calling us to do, we discover that our Heavenly Father didn't ask us to jump so we could drown. He has a plan to prosper us and not to harm us. When we jump, we put ourselves in a position where our faith can grow, but if you don't ever jump, you'll never have that experience. You don't need perfect faith to be used greatly by God; you need enough to respond in obedience. You need enough faith to jump.

For some, God is trying to coax you into the pool; He's trying to get you to jump! He's saying, "Don't be afraid . . . don't be afraid . . . don't be afraid. Trust me even though it's scary, even though it doesn't make sense, even though you don't know where the journey may lead. If you'll trust me and jump, you'll come to discover that I can be trusted. But if you don't obey, you'll never know."

For me and Laura, the journey all started with me sitting at a conference and God nudging me to trust him and step out on faith to start a church. We were unqualified and under resourced. We had our baggage and issues and levels of dysfunction like everyone else. We had no idea how to start a church, but realized, "That's not our problem. We need to be the "who" and we will let God worry about the "how" and so we jumped.

All God needed was for two unlikely people to step out in faith. He knew how to impact a community. And often when I'm speaking on the weekend and looking out at the faces of the people in attendance or when I'm reading an email of a life that has been changed through the ministry of Hope Community Church, I think, "What if we hadn't jumped? Imagine all that we would have missed."

What is God asking you to do? Where in your life is God saying, "Jump!"—but you're afraid? Step out in faith. Trust Him for the journey. With God's power, push past the doubts and fears that hold you back . . . and jump. You have no idea where God will take you or how He will use you. If He can use us, why not you? You can't, but God can.

About the Author

Mike Lee is the founding and lead pastor of Hope Community Church in the Raleigh, North Carolina area. He has been teaching the Bible for over 35 years in a dynamic, relevant and insightful way. His desire is that people come to know and love Jesus and be renewed in their minds through God's Word. He and his wife, Laura, have two sons, two daughters-in-law and seven grandchildren.

ABOOKS

ALIVE Book Publishing and ALIVE Publishing Group
are imprints of Advanced Publishing LLC,
3200 A Danville Blvd., Suite 204, Alamo, California 94507

Telephone: 925.837.7303
alivebookpublishing.com

CPSIA information can be obtained
at www.ICGtesting.com
Printed in the USA
LVHW04s0052210418
574338LV00001BB/1/P